Praise for
The Sacred Flight of the Teenager

"Parenting a teenager is full of challenges, and letting go may be the hardest. In *The Sacred Flight of the Teenager,* Dr. Susan Smith Kuczmarski helps parents see how, how much, and when to get out of the way of a teen who is getting ready to soar. The wonderful thing is that her book will lift you up too!"

Donald A. Baker, Executive Director, Youth Organizations Umbrella, Inc.

"If I were parenting a teenager again, I would keep one copy of Susan's book by my bedside and another in my car. I only wish that as a parent, I had been able to have access to her insights to guide me through those difficult periods. I would love to give a copy to every parent that I know upon his or her child's graduation from elementary school."

Catherine F. Beadles, Teacher/Gifted and Talented Program, Aiken County, South Carolina, Public Schools

"How my husband and I wish we'd had this book while raising our teens! I give it rave reviews! It's rich with humor and sensitivity, empathy and understanding. I love how the author sees the kids' as well as the parents' side."

Dottie Billington, Ph.D., author of *Life Is an Attitude*

"I read *The Sacred Flight* the same week my older son got his driving permit and my younger son turned 13. It was a timely palliative for the new confusions and self-doubts I've been experiencing in the early teen years. Mothering little ones was a 'natural' for me; but these teenagers are a foreign breed! *The Sacred Flight* is a practical, reassuring, easily digestible guide for navigating this foreign territory of teenagerhood."

Beth Brooks, Director, Office of the President/ Colorado College

"It is very helpful to parents to hear advice from those who have had or are having experiences with their own teens. Dr. Susan Smith Kuczmarski combines her expertise as educator and parent in an engaging and positive way. The notion of respecting the teenager for who he or she is during a time for self-discovery is brought out in this book. Parents will learn that offering patience, guidance, and a firm stand are important and possible."

Linda Campbell, 8th Grade Teacher/Chicago City Day School

"For those confronting the trying if not treacherous terrain of parenting teenagers, there is hope. The author confidently guides us through developmental passages in order to overcome the trials of these turbulent years, arriving at child-parent relationships that can survive, even thrive."

Michelle Moeller Chandler, Ph.D., Educator—Williams College, Williamstown, Mass.

"Susan Smith Kuczmarski has written a very insightful, essential, and invaluable book for parents, to guide them in their efforts to have a healthy, living relationship with their ever changing, challenging, and demanding adolescent children. Kuczmarski, a parent herself of two teens and one pre-teen, helps other parents avoid becoming micromanagers of their teens' lives. Instead, she clearly and succinctly states the ways in which parents can fulfill their roles as caring, compassionate, supportive parents with immense love and utmost regard for their soon-to-be-adult children."

Henry Doyle, Priest, Chaplain & Religious Studies Department Chair—Shatuck—Saint Mary's School

"The greatest gift, as parents, to our children and the world is to steward with invisible strings of love and permission. *The Sacred Flight of the Teenager* will be your very best friend as you let go, without ever leaving their hearts behind . . . or yours!!

Nancy Drew, author of *The Artful Spirit* and *First-Aid Kit for Mothers*

"The concepts contained in this book are very timely for today's parents. Dr. Kuczmarski's recommendations are easily incorporated into the real lives of both teens and parents without having to change their lives upside-down. It gives options that are empowering to all parties involved. I would recommend this book to parents who would like to 'get real' with their teens."

Jennie Hernandez Hanks, author of *A Little Secret for Dealing with Teens*

"As the parent of a teenager and two pre-teens, the information and thought process outlined will really come in handy. This book will be a good starting point in the maturation of the family unit."

Kenneth Polin, M.D., Pediatrician, Children's Memorial Hospital, Northwestern University Medical Center

"This book is chock full of excellent information all parents of teens need. And it is simultaneously nourishing and encouraging for the reader. . . . I highly recommend this book for parents of teens or anyone who is dealing with a teen on their own challenging process. The book is a model for making room for the 'other' in relationships."

Kathryn Sain, M.A., Clinical Psychologist

"Dr. Susan Smith Kuczmarski's endlessly readable book *The Sacred Flight of the Teenager* places emphasis on the uniqueness of every teenager and how valuable that discovery can be. Within these short, humorous chapters is a gold mine of valuable information to provide the bridge between you and your teenager."

Kimberly Senior, Resident Artist/Steppenwolf Theatre Company

"The author's sensitive approach, coupled with insightful exercises, result in an easy-to-read book, full of tools that have practical application for day-to-day family life. As owners of a program where a child's physical and emotional needs are central, we feel this book has an abundance of important suggestions and reflections and is a must-read for any individual working with children."

Jim and Donna Stein, Owners and Directors of The Road Less Traveled

"Dr. Kuczmarski uses humor, as well as personal and professional insight, to guide parents of teenagers through the art of walking the fine line of stepping back, without stepping out."

Michelle L. Trujillo, author of *Why Can't We Talk? What Teens Would Share If Parents Would Listen* and *Teens Talkin' Faith*

"Behind Susan Kuczmarski's helpful ideas on how to effectively parent a teenager is a profound faith in the human spirit that longs for and naturally guides itself toward self-preservation and self-realization. Much like the flower that grows to catch the sun, she believes teenagers will pursue the path that best leads them to their own light. Her book inspired me to trust that belief."

Chrissy Washburn, Mental Health Counselor/ Portland, Oregon

"Parenting teens today is not 'business as usual.' Not only are the times significantly different than merely a decade ago, so is what teens need to traverse a world that requires a great deal of psychological hardiness—which is precisely why *The Sacred Flight of the Teenager* is not only a timely book, but an important one. This book will help you equip your teenager with skills to make sound choices in a new and remarkably challenging world."

Bettie B. Youngs, Ph.D, author of *Taste Berries for Teens* series

ALSO BY SUSAN SMITH KUCZMARSKI, ED.D.

The Family Bond:
Inspiring Tips for Creating a Closer Family

Values-Based Leadership
(with Tom Kuczmarski)

The Sacred Flight of the Teenager

A Parent's Guide to Stepping Back and Letting Go

SUSAN SMITH KUCZMARSKI, Ed.D.

BOOK ENDS PUBLISHING
Chicago

Cover design by Bruce Swart
Interior illustrations by Robert Wilmott

Published by Book Ends Publishing
2001 N. Halsted St, Suite 201
Chicago, Illinois 60614
www.sacredflight.com

Catalog-in-Publication data available from the Library of Congress.

Printed in the United States of America.
International Standard Book Number: 0-9677817-3-6

To Thomas D. Kuczmarski,
for his good nature, sense of humor, humility, and constancy;
to our three sons, John, James, and Thomas,
who shared their "flight" path;
and in memory of John R. Cooper, Ph.D.,
treasured friend, psychologist, and loving spirit

CONTENTS

ACKNOWLEDGMENTS

I am enormously grateful to my husband, Tom, who lent his wisdom, encouragement, and support at every phase of this book; to my generous friend, Beth Ylvisaker, for her kindness, sunshine, guiding strength, and involvement in our own family's journey; to Kim Grant who edited each draft with a remarkable combination of precision and warmth; to Robert Wilmott, who created the line drawings with imagination and humor; to Josefina Aguayo who graciously and effeciently took command of numerous administrative matters related to book production; to Rich Hagle for his wealth of knowledge related to all aspects of publishing; to Jeremy Cohen for his seasoned director's eye and exceptional guidance; to the open, committed parents and teens who were interviewed for this project, especially to Suzanne Pelton; to a small group of supportive women with whom I have a deep and enduring bond: Martha Donovan, Colleen Dudgeon-Ransdell, Reven Fellars, Marina Gorey, Barbara Habas, Tracy Hurst, Sally Parsons, Erica Regunberg, and Christina Van Pelt; and finally, to my own parents, Fernando and Bula Smith, who provided freedom, laughter, and a spirit of giving along my own teenage "flight" path.

Get Ready for the Ride

Parenting a teenager is an act of courage. It requires great effort, deep caring, knowing that the stakes are high, enduring pain—great pain—and letting go. The teenage struggle and focus carries enormous lessons for everyone involved. The family is in a precarious position during the teen years. Although the child-turned-teen continues to need the loving support of a close family, family life now seems a "drag," a burden, an outright embarrassment to the independence-seeking teen.

The relationship between you and your teen needs to undergo a major shift now, if it is to live. As dependence gives way to independence, boundaries—and limits—are pushed out. A teen's inner world opens, even explodes, and a phase of great expansion begins. Lots of space is needed. The transition, at times, will not be pretty.

Parenting a teen is not a linear experience. You don't start at point A, then go to point B, and continue through to Z. There is no recipe or orderly step-by-step approach to take with teens. It's more like taking a jigsaw puzzle out of its box, seeing all the pieces

mixed up and upside down—and discovering that there is no helpful picture on the lid to help you put the puzzle together. Many parents feel lost during this period. They don't see that the best
approach may often be to simply "step back." Yet slowly, piece by
piece, we discover and learn.

The Sacred Flight of the Teenager will help you piece together
a workable understanding of the puzzling teenage years and,
hopefully, catch a glimpse of the beautiful big picture that is even
now emerging. This collection of forty individual essays is loosely
organized around five topics: letting go, keeping in touch, exploring, acquiring skills, and connecting. *The Sacred Flight of the
Teenager* can serve as a guide and companion for this wild last ride
together—one in which you will weep in painful confusion and
smile with delight as your teen becomes an adult.

PART 1

Letting Go

1

The Sacred Step

There is something inherently sacred about the lives of teenagers. In their passage from childhood to adulthood, a new adult life forms and emerges for all to see. The family, because it nurtures human life and helps it form, is also sacred. Your work is to create in your home a sanctuary of love, nurturing, and support. . . . Sounds great, doesn't it? But it's far from easy. Because while you're putting your heartfelt energy into creating this loving home environment, your teen is probably telling you, in hundreds of ways, that he doesn't even want to be near you anymore. You can't bail out now (tempting as it is) because your teen needs your love—perhaps more than ever. So you must love and let go—simultaneously. To love, you will have to somehow hang in there for them. To let go, keep reminding yourself: "This is not

about me." This may be the hardest thing you've ever done as a parent.

Your teen is detaching now. This is a natural part of the process of family life. The need to detach is so great that your teen may not even talk to you for long periods of time. He may avoid you altogether. In fact, much of his bizarre behavior can be explained with an eye on this desire to detach. Don't hold on. Don't try to control. Stop acting as if you know best. He has his own ideas and programs and plans. Get out of the way. His life must move forward now. Your teen is preparing to take a sacred step— discovering an adult self. And you need to step back.

As one mother so aptly shared, "At some pivotal point, a

teen's life has nothing to do with you. They are so consumed by the job of getting to adulthood that they can hardly acknowledge that you exist. During this time, they simply don't take in that other people have needs or that it would be a good idea to do something for another person because that's a nice thing to do. It's just not part of their thinking right now."

You are being asked not to play the primary role at this time. Your teen wants to separate from you. Yes, your formerly loving and adorable child will now be saying, "Get out of my life." It is not a clean, swift break, as you will see from my interviews. The pain can be excruciating and all-encompassing. But it is the right move. It is also an opportunity to express a deep generosity. Find comfort in knowing that letting go is a gift—the ultimate expression of a generous heart.

It's time to detach. It's not good-bye—just time to move onward to something new. Trust in the light. It will get brighter. Your days will be colorful again. For now, get out of the way. Honor the distance.

Sacredness coexists with pain while
your teen is detaching.

2

Pain

"I was dumped by my son. It was awful. My heart was breaking. Nobody told me that this could happen . . . "

—mother of a teen

It may seem like your teen is rejecting you. He is. Young children can give you the greatest amount of love in your life—maybe more than you've ever received. So when they become teenagers, and their rejection is proportionately as large, it can feel like a gloomy farewell indeed. And all sorts of personal issues—like your own self-esteem, unfinished business from your family of origin, and all-too familiar past family dynamics—come up. A teen's rejection may even appear cruel. Here's how one parent describes this pain:

"It is terrible pain because you still love them to death, but you can see how it is that some parents kick their teens out. They're so awful, so rude and so self-absorbed. I think they stop listening to you after about age twelve and then you have to find other ways of communicating with them. But when they turn you off, it's like a whole piece of your heart dies because you still like them and want to be part of their lives . . . ."

One mother confided:

"Oh, and let there be a crisis in your family, and you really need help from your teen . . . nothing . . . nothing . . . be desperate, be ill, have a death in the family, you have to move. Any of those crises that come along, and ask your teenager, 'I understand, honey, that you're expressing yourself, but I need your help right now. I need you, could you just do this for me' . . . nothing. The more you need them, the less available they are. They will just not be needed by you. It's bizarre."

Teens need their parents to be less involved in their lives. There is simply less room for family, and this is a painful fact for most parents, as described below:

"He didn't want to have anything to do with us then, and it was too sharp. He's kind of back in our lives now. We kind of do things. He still doesn't need to see us very much, but he comes back and forth, and he borrows some things and we give him things or encourage him to make a doctor appointment or something like that, but he really just wants to sleep and be with his friends."

If you call him and say, "Hey, can you come over?" what happens? This same parent says:

"He doesn't. In fact I said to him when he came last, 'You know it would be really nice for Grace (his little sister) to see you. You could think about coming over at least once a week. You know, I'll make dinner and . . . .' His response was that he's tired from his job and he wants to hang out with his friends and he isn't going to factor in a dinner once a week with his parents. That's just not important to him."

The pain of separation is intense. Know that it is necessary. Try not to take your teen's behavior too personally. An adult is emerging from deep within the teen—opening to his or her unique destiny. One mother that I interviewed had the following to say about this destiny: "I really believe that children come into this world with something—an agenda of their own that has nothing to do with me. Each one of them has something they are meant to be doing in this world, and they have to figure out what that is. Maybe if I look hard or carefully at my daughter, I'll see what that is and nurture it, whatever it is."

The pain of separation can be intense as our teenagers grow into their individual destinies.

3

The Art of Argument

"The only thing I remember about my oldest son being a teenager is that we argued a lot. It was so bad that from boarding school, instead of saying, 'I'm going to call home,' he said, 'I'm going to call dial-an-argument.' One time, all the way to the airport to pick him up, my mantra was, 'It takes two people to have an argument. If I don't open my mouth, we can't argue, and if I don't say anything, we'll be fine.' And we were in the midst of a horrible, knock-down argument before I could get out of the parking lot."

—parent of a teenager

Why are teens so argumentative? They are busy practicing a new way of thinking. (Jean Piaget called it "formal operational thought.") Between eleven and sixteen years of age, teens

develop the ability to solve problems without the concrete, action-oriented experiences of a child. Teens are forming theories about everything—and testing them out. They make assumptions, consider hypotheses, and work out the inferences that follow. This abstract thinking is actually very difficult to master. So, teens argue constantly to practice their abstract thought processes.

Most parents are threatened by their arguing teen. I know of one dad who threatened to put his argumentative daughter into juvenile hall because of it. She was a totally good kid with straight A's, piano recitals, drama club—the whole bit. If he'd understood that she was struggling to learn abstract thought and logic, perhaps lively debates would have taken the place of rejection and heartbreak on their home front.

What can parents do to actively support their teen's abstract thinking? Why not go with the flow and nurture this new development? Encourage your teen's efforts to define his or her world view through abstraction and reflection, questioning, and experimentation. Don't rush in with answers. And don't automatically go on the war path when a teenager questions your most dearly held values or assumptions about life. Let teens have the opportunity to make intellectual choices for themselves. Organize your home environment to allow for formal abstract thinking.

Why not create a think tank in your home that is enriching, both socially and intellectually? Let your teens interact with other people's views. Expose them to different types of people and ideas—different role models too. Dig out some of your old college books on logic. Reread Aristotle and Socrates. Introduce them to your teen. (Wow! They'll think you're "far out.") You might even set up and engage in formal debates. (This would have the added benefit of teaching all of you the rules for "fighting fair" when you disagree.) Remember: the goal is to increase the capacity to think—for teens and parents alike. So, use this time to reexamine some of your own ideas and clean up any of your own thought processes that may have grown rigid, rusty, or sloppy over time. The timing is perfect to support your teen's cognitive growth—and your own.

*Know that this argumentative phase is related to
your teen's struggle to learn abstract thought and logic.
Try to nurture, support, and even enjoy this development,
rather than feel annoyed or threatened by it.*

4

Tai Chi

A friend on the West coast suggested that I do some reading on Taoism because my writing used some of its themes. Next thing I know, I'm hooked. Taoism is an ancient philosophy of living in balance, in harmony with nature. It's not about trying to get something or somewhere: It's about acceptance. Taoism teaches that wisdom lies in not contending. The secret is to allow things to take their natural course. The message for parents is clear: Don't fight against the current, flow with it. If we parents can learn to stand back, our teens will move ahead, following their own inner nature. Often, parents lead most effectively by permitting teens to be their own guides.

Taoist thought says to let negative forces pass you—and to return love. I think this is one of the most helpful strategies for

parents: Meet hostility with kindness. While the oncoming force from your teen (e.g., bad words or "attitude") started out as an attempt to reach out to you, it became filtered or tainted when it passed through your teen's personality. Your teen's love became distorted. One must learn to look past the teen's (or opponent's) personality and see pure love coming towards you, maintain your center, and, as hard as it may be—return love. Taoist thought says: Produce the right loving action at the right time. Timing is everything.

Tai chi is a martial art that comes out of Taoism. It expresses Taoist principles through the beautiful, flowing movements of the practitioner's body. When I take my walks in the morning, I always see a man practicing tai chi, his body, arms and legs swaying in rhythmic harmony. The movement in tai chi is generated not so much in the forced exertion of muscle strength as in the consciously directed flow of chi (energy). Chi circulates through the entire body and enables one to move with ease and power. With every move, the body appears to be light and agile. Grace, balance, and timing are critical in tai chi—just as they are in relating to teens.

In tai chi, force (i.e., muscle strength) doesn't matter. To overcome the strong—one must yield. Parents can learn to yield to a teen's oncoming force or blow—whether verbal (e.g., a nasty comment), psychic (e.g., mentally cruel treatment), or even physical (e.g., a misplaced fist)—and stay centered, retaining their dignity and equilibrium. Here's how: Practitioners of tai chi strive to avoid something called "double-weightedness." This is your state when your weight is evenly distributed on both feet, and movement doesn't flow freely. To prevent it, tai chi uses the technique of stepping backward as the opponent advances, then stepping forward as the opponent retreats. This is the little sapling's stance as it bends to accept the windy fury of the storm and survives, while the old oak, rigid and immense, is violently uprooted. Don't be like the stationary oak, resistant and static. Rather, step back. This will help you weather the tempest as your teen storms into adulthood.

Practitioners of tai chi believe that one should bear oneself like the eagle that glides peacefully on the wind—until the instant it plunges from the sky to snatch a fish from the river far below. The eagle's restful alertness and its capacity for swift, decisive action are traits we parents do well to emulate. Waysun Liao in *T'ai Chi Classics* describes it this way: "When in stillness, you should feel as if you are a mountain: stable, peaceful, formidable, being yourself. When you are in motion, you should move and feel like the waters of a river: roaring ceaselessly, yielding to any condition, capable of being both peaceful and powerful." The message for parents is to stay balanced. Keep a clear, centered mind. Conserve, rather than expend, your chi (energy). Then, when you need to engage the roaring river or the striking eagle, your chi will be available to you. You have stored your strength for later use.

Keep in mind these images from tai chi. Discover the hidden power of the young sapling's nonresistance. And, in the restful stillness of the gliding eagle or the silent mountain, conserve your power and energy for use when it is truly required. Practice the art of yielding and of peacefully storing your energy, engaging it when there is a need to respond swiftly and powerfully.

Let the lessons of Taoism and tai chi inform your parenting. Lead by letting teens follow their own nature and be their own guides. Step back and allow negative force to pass by you; then return love. Conserve your energy for when you really need it.

5

On Stepping In and Stepping Back (and When to Do Which)

Many parents asked me where to draw the line between getting involved and stepping back. If physical harm is a possibility, then the line should be quickly and cleanly drawn. When drugs, guns, alcohol abuse, drinking and driving, or other types of dangerous or illegal behaviors are involved, plunge in like the eagle—and fast! But consider the value of taking the sapling's gentle, more yielding approach on much of the other "stuff" with your teen.

Instead of jumping in or freaking out, it may be best to simply remain silent—even smile. Sometimes we can help the most by doing nothing—or very little. If parents just charge in without thinking, fireworks can erupt and shoot dangerously off course before anyone even knows what's happened. More times than I'd like to admit, I have made the mistake of stepping forward, getting involved, talking too much, and expressing what I thought was the best approach—only to wish later that I'd just kept my mouth shut.

Beware of overinvolvement. Try smiles and humor instead. You might even experiment with treating your teen as if he were someone else's! This can enable you to relate to him with more objectivity and lightheartedness. One father used this tactic with a troublesome issue and shared the following success story with me: An odor that filled the room as his son arrived home late one night provided strong evidence that his teen had been smoking cigarettes. A typical parental response to this would be something like: "You've been smoking! You can't do that! It will ruin your health—and your life! I want you to stop it right now!" Instead, this father simply stated, "You smell like a smoke stack," to which the son replied, "Guess I forgot to open the flue." In a lighthearted way, he had confronted his son and let him know that he was aware of the smoking. Then, at a later time, when the teen was less vulnerable (i.e., the following morning), the father might remind him how difficult it is to stop, how quickly addiction sets in, and how awful it is healthwise (perhaps playing on the son's interests in sports, as the father in our story ended up doing).

A close friend of mine shared her approach with me. Rather than yelling at her son for breaking her car CD player, she told him that when she inserted her classical music, the player rejected it because it had decided that it now only wants to listen to his rock

music. He got the point. She effectively used lightheartedness rather than anger.

Just recently, I told myself to smile when my son moved his entire set of weights into the middle of the room where I write. Their unannounced arrival on my office floor that day had transformed my serene writing space into a makeshift gym. At first, I even worried that the sheer weight of all this equipment would cause the ceiling to collapse into our bedroom below. But rather than get all huffy-puffy, I told myself to be flexible, smile, live with the weights for a short while, and see what happened. Sure enough, as quickly as they had appeared, they vanished—into an exercise area out back. I effortlessly regained my writing space by taking a lighthearted approach.

*Jump in fast when your teen is in big trouble—
but practice lightheartedness and use humor
for the smaller stuff.*

6

A Feast of Laughter

One sect of Zen Buddhists begin their mornings with fifteen minutes of laughter; they say that the remainder of their day then falls naturally into its proper place. The power of laughter is so great that there is even value in faking it. A good laugh not only gives quick energy but also lets the body relax and release stress. Think of something that at first appears negative and try to see the humor in it. Even poke fun at yourself. Recall and share it with another parent. Don't leave humor and merriment to the comedians. Life with teens is too tumultuous for that. Balance all that angst and intensity with the power of laughter and the joy of play.

You may want to keep a story book and record your family's

wacky adventures. Recalling these when times are too serious can bring in some frivolity and a fresh perspective when you need it most. Here's an entry from our family's journal of outrageous adventures:

> When one of our sons was fourteen, we had a most unusual Thanksgiving Day "feast." Preparation for the big meal was moving along very smoothly. The bird was stuffed and cooking in the oven, when one of our teens went over to the stove. He began to play with the oven door—and accidentally locked it! Most ovens have this lock feature, which is used when the oven is cleaned. On this particular oven, once the door is locked, the clean cycle begins. Period. Clean time is preset for three hours. During this time, oven temperature is extremely high, and it is impossible to open the door. The oven temperature must drop to a safe level before the door can be unlocked.
>
> Once we realized that our oven had entered the cleaning mode, we panicked. We tried to unlock the door using force, but only succeeded in jamming it and damaging the lock mechanism. Without a doubt, our bird was now captive in the self-cleaning oven.
>
> We rushed to a nearby grocery store, just five minutes before closing time, and purchased a fresh, large turkey breast and drumstick to put on the outside grill. Within forty minutes, our second-string turkey dinner was cooked and ready for all to enjoy. The next morning I called Jerry's Oven and Range Repair, whose ad I found in the yellow pages. Over the phone, he taught me how to fix the jammed lock. It

took three tries, but finally the handle moved back into place, and our shrunken, dried-up turkey emerged from captivity.

While this event caused some tense moments, we still laugh at the experience. Now, at every Thanksgiving, friends ask us if our bird made it out of the oven OK. We smile back and recall the experience with a mixture of joy and uncertainty. You just never know what's going to happen. . . .

A good sense of humor is an essential
tool for surviving the teenage years.
Develop it, use it—and share it!

7

Superteen Takes Flight

Idealism and vitality—nothing watered down. Witness the appearance of Superteen! Infused with passion and charged with energy, Superteen plunges into life with urgency and impatience. Just as Clark Kent sheds his business suit and tie for the familiar red and blue Superman cape, your teen sheds her childhood role to take on a new identity. Stepping into what she thinks she wants to be, she needs space to grow and make mistakes. A dancer, a cartoonist, scientist, musician, or beautician—she won't know for sure yet. She is in a state of becoming. She is fearless now. She is a visionary. She is might.

Superteen is a powerful force, with experimentation and risk-taking as her creed. Adorned with green spiked hair and a blemished fearless face, Superteen takes flight on weekend nights. A beat-up car—trashed with crinkled school notebooks, old food, and messy clothes—is superteen's flying machine. In it, Superteen travels everywhere. She drives recklessly, runs the streets at all hours, and walks on the bad side of town, impervious to any sense of danger.

When *your* Superteen takes flight—when passionate risk-taking and dynamic restlessness seem to overpower all common sense—what can you do? Make sure your teen has accurate information, offer a safety net, and pray. Let me explain.

Give accurate information. Initiate frequent discussions to help Superteen make safe choices about drinking and drugs. Give your teen the most accurate and up-to-date information you can about the dangers, health risks, and legal consequences. Do the same with regard to sex and the risks of unwanted pregnancies, sexually transmitted diseases, and the subtler emotional and relational problems that can result from jumping carelessly into sex. Read and keep informed. Then, have realistic conversations with teens—not to scare them—but to help them make safe decisions. Seeking fun and living passionately in the present dominate teenage thinking. But a loving voice of reason, accurate information, and sensible caution can help to counterbalance your teen's wild side.

Extend a safety net. Tell your teenager something like, "If you're ever in a situation, day or night, where you're in trouble, call me. I won't ask any questions. I'll come and give you and your friends a ride home. No questions asked. If you ever need anything, know that you can count on me." Be a safety net to catch

them when their need is extreme or urgent. Be sure they know they can call you *any time.*

Don't worry . . . Pray! Kick the worry habit. Instead, put the power of prayer to work in guiding and protecting your son or daughter. Ask God for help. Ask a guardian angel—or a whole legion of angels!—to watch over your teen. Surround your teen (and all your loved ones, for that matter) with the healing and protective power of your loving prayers.

As Superteen takes flight, offer accurate information, hold out a safety net —and pray!

8

Turtle Medicine

A friend gave me a smooth brown agate with a turtle carved on it. I keep it on my desk and look at it often to remind myself that, like the earthy turtle, I must become masterful at the art of grounding. Turtle medicine is essential now—as your teen takes flight.

Keep your feet on the ground. Stay close to the earth. You need this partnership. Connect with nature. It may be your best antidote to the wild, risk-taking teen. I take daily walks around a nearby pond. Even if I have to leave our house at 6:00 a.m., I try not to miss a day—rain, snow, or sunshine. It nourishes my senses and gives me balance—like the turtle with all four feet on the earthly soil.

Remain sturdy, even when carrying great weights. Expect

good and bad times. Focus on being solid, strong, robust. The load will become lighter with time. The turtle's message is clear: Remain centered, patient. When you feel frazzled, think of the turtle, on all fours, sitting in the sun or shade, completely connected to Mother Earth. Gather your thoughts gently "under your shell" and reconnect with stillness and the part of you that is connected with the earth.

Be patient. The turtle reminds us to take things slowly. Fruit that is harvested too soon is bitter and hard, but given the opportunity to ripen, its inborn sweetness emerges. Your teen is likewise ripening and maturing. Don't hurry the process. Surrender to this time. Sink into the joy of the moment. Relax and try to have fun with your teen. Don't worry about doing it right. If you make a mistake, learn from it. The fruit is better when it has ripened slowly on the tree.

Protect yourself. If your teen is attacking or threatening you or making you feel hostile or angry, try the turtle's way. When danger threatens, a turtle will simply withdraw its exposed head, tail, and legs into its shell. As parents, sometimes it's best to withdraw into our shells and wait out the siege. Later, when the attack is over, we can take action to prevent it from happening again. Know that the turtle's protective shell has a lot to do with its longevity. (Turtles have been around for 200 million years, since the time when dinosaurs roamed the earth.) Your longevity may depend on knowing how to retreat too.

Rest. The passage to adulthood is arduous for your teen—and fatiguing for you. Rest is essential for parents. Picture the turtle tucking in its head, legs, and tail to hibernate in the mud—or soaking up sunshine while resting on a rock. Keep in mind that just as the turtle buries its eggs in the sand and allows the sun to hatch the little ones, you too can step out of the way and refocus on yourself. Take breaks, even vacations from your teens.

Keep your feet on the ground, like the turtle,
and stay close to the earth. Remain sturdy and centered.
Be patient. Learn to withdraw, when necessary.
And be sure to get adequate rest.

PART 2

Keeping In Touch

9

※

The Wisdom of Goats

Last summer, a neighbor brought over several farm animals to join our family: a chicken named "Noodle" (who astonishingly layed blue eggs!), a bunny named "Bugs," and a goat named "Lisa." Of the three, it was the goat who fit most easily into our family scene—and provided me with many valuable insights into the workings of teenage minds.

If we would all line up, our goat's favorite was our oldest teenage son, John. While we would all take Lisa for walks, John was her preferred shepherd. I think it was because he gave her the most freedom. Shortly after taking her along the walking path, he removed her leash and let her roam about wherever she pleased. The goat knew John consistently gave her this freedom to move about. Her short tail would turn upward and wave every time she saw him. Like goats, teens want and enjoy freedom too. They react extremely positively to times when they know you've granted them a walk on the "wilder" side of life. John understood Lisa's yearning to roam free, and this, I believe, formed the basis for the strong bond between them.

While there were many interesting behaviors associated with Lisa the Goat, her water-drinking pattern was especially relevant to our discussion of teens. Since the summer days were hot, replenishing her supply of water, we thought, was especially important. (This focus no doubt went back to losing a hamster, who died of "overheat" and "underwater" five years earlier under similar weather conditions.) So we always kept a concerned eye on our goat's water dish. Much to our surprise, she consistently knocked it over. During the course of a day, we'd fill it up again and again, only to find it all dumped out the next time we checked.

What we had here was a serious conflict in values! What was important to us was clearly not important to this goat. Now, Lisa the Goat never knew of our family's tragic loss of Scotty the Hamster due to dehydration. If she had, she might have been a bit more compassionate with our inordinate concern with filling her water bowl. Yet she did, on some level, sense that something in our past was clouding our perception of her in the present—a situation she did everything in her power to rectify. Let's not make the same mistake with our teens! If we take the time to get clear on their values, and incorporate this understanding into our interactions with them, our lives will work a lot more smoothly.

*A little attention to a teen's values early on can
save a lot of head-butting down the road.*

10

Values

A value is what is important to a person—what is cherished and believed in. Values influence the choices we make, the way we invest our energy and time, the people we choose to be close to, and the interests we pursue. In difficult times, they serve as a compass amid conflicting demands and varying points of view. To lay a foundation for a life that is real, meaningful, and satisfying, we must know exactly what our personal values are. The starting point for our journey through life with teens is a basic awareness of values and the forces that shape them.

Teens have their own unique values, and it is very important to let them surface. It might be helpful to have your teen write down his values. Write yours down too. And share them with each other. A note of extreme caution: Don't try to impose *your* values onto your teen! Teens must discover, identify, and own their val-

ues—and not simply replicate ours. Although this identification process sounds simple, it requires some serious thinking and reflection for teen and adult alike. A few guidelines for parents are helpful: Recognize the intrinsic value, strengths, and merit of your teen's values; acknowledge and support the values cited by your teen; and encourage open discussions on the topic of values.

Let me share with you what happened several years ago when our teenage sons, our ten-year-old, my husband, and I sat by the fire one cold, snowy night and wrote down our individual values. (Both teenagers identified freedom as a key value, as you will see from their lists below.) Our sixteen-year-old, John, valued honesty, kindness, happiness and joy, close relationships with great friends and family, belief in oneself, perseverance, balance and yin/yang, knowledge and experience, purity, individuality, good health, and freedom; he likes nature, the ocean, computers, and the rush and excitement of surfing, karate, and running. Our fourteen-year-old, James, valued swing dancing, friends, family, beaches, hot breakfast, laughing, reading a good book, listening to music, and freedom, which he describes as "the ability and pre-rogative to make his own decisions." Our ten-year-old, Thomas, valued basketball, the ocean, legos, friends, winter, and J.R.R. Tolkien stuff. My husband valued respect and consideration for others, belief in diversity, the power of love, trust, family, individu-ality, and self-esteem. I valued time for relaxation, no stress, deep friendships, nature, family fun and togetherness, intimate conver-sations, deep self-reflection, and spiritual understanding.

Have each member of your family list his or her own individual values. Then, each person should try to select five top values and write them down. Have each family member talk about his or her values with everyone listening deeply.

Understanding your teen's values creates greater harmony in a family. There is awareness and clarity on what's important to each family member. Parents can use this information to help plan what to do with free time, weekends, and vacations in order to tap into a teen's interests.

If a teenager has clearly identified her values, she will be bet-ter able to handle the ups and downs along life's journey. With val-ues in place, a teen will have greater comfort when taking risks, because she knows what is deeply important to her. She will see what interests outweigh others and will be stronger because of it. By being aware of her values, she will know what is significant to her and will be able to have greater involvement in, and control over, her life choices.

Encourage teens to identify and prioritize their values—
then share them as a family, if possible.

11

Changing Values

"Who Are You?" said the caterpillar. Alice replied rather shyly, "I . . . I hardly know sir, just at present—at least I know who I was when I got up this morning, but I must have changed several times since then."

—Lewis Caroll in *Alice in Wonderland*

One of our sons threw a party while we were away for a night. He assured and promised us, half a dozen times at least, that no person would come into our house while we were away. When he told us on the evening of our return that twenty-three friends had come over, I uncalmly said to him, "I've lost the sense of trust we had. How do you explain this after you told us so many times that no one would walk into our house?" He answered: "I've changed since I told you that several days ago, and giving parties

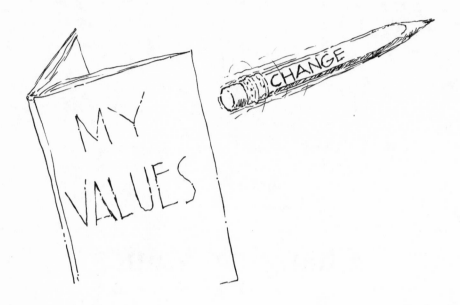

with my friends is now really important to me." While we didn't buy it or let him off the hook, we did learn how quickly teens change their views, and how important and difficult it is to keep up with them. Change is rampant, wild, and unpredictable in a teen, much like Alice described in her Wonderland.

Keeping up with the changing values of a teen is sort of like trying to catch a train after it's already left the station. But we owe it to them—and to ourselves—to give it a try. Values evolve over time in response to the forces of life. Some of these forces are stubborn and relentless—like our goat's constant dumping of her water dish. Others are sudden, almost shattering. Still others are so gentle and subtle that we scarcely notice them.

Think about your own values. What is their origin? How did they come about? How have they changed? Four factors shape our values: (1) family and childhood experiences, (2) personal relationships with significant individuals, (3) major life changes and learning experiences, and (4) conflict events that produce self-discovery. These factors, combined with our own learning and self-discovery, transform our values over time. Let's take a close look at each.

1. Family and childhood experiences. During childhood, parents, family members, siblings, peers, teachers, and religious organizations share their beliefs and shape our values. Our childhood experiences from school, family rituals, holidays and celebrations, travel and vacations, as well as daily family practices, styles of interaction, and approaches to discipline—all work together to form our core values.

2. Personal relationships with significant individuals. There are a handful of individuals that we meet in our daily lives who really "connect" with us. Teachers, school friends, bosses, current buddies, or older persons can all be special role models whom we look up to, respect, admire, and want to emulate. These special people's values will greatly influence the formation of our own.

3. Major life changes and learning experiences. Marriage, rearing children, taking a new job or position, moving to a new geographic location, confronting the death of a significant other, or adjusting to the departure of children from home—all cause our values to shift and evolve over time. Discovering new motivations, emotions, and conflicts within ourselves can bring new light to old beliefs that we have always taken for granted. Learning more about ourselves, others, and how to deal with different people invites us to examine and reinvent our values. For example, an adolescent's first love relationship can often open up huge new avenues to self-discovery.

4. Conflict events. Wars, environmental disasters, community crime, government programs, legal reforms, and other sources of societal, or externally-driven, conflict often transform our values in deep and lasting ways. Divorce, job loss, school failures, loss of a partner, hurtful friends, or an unwanted pregnancy—these personally-driven conflicts bring us up short and exert yet another kind of pressure on our values. We must all come to terms with conflict experiences, and learn from them.

For teens and adults alike—life is full of forces that cause us to examine and reexamine our values as we travel on our way.

Teen's values are changing rapidly. Do your best to
stay aware and keep in touch.

12

Hello In There

"Why does she (my mother) think she knows anything about me?"

—a teenager

A lot of teens I interviewed told me that their parents don't really know them. These teens wanted to be recognized and loved for "who I am inside." Parents often get hung up on physical appearance—if teens have a pierced earring or pink hair or strange clothing—and miss the inner essence of their teens. As one mother said, "We're not paying attention to who they are inside. And that's what they want more than anything."

How do you get to know who your teen really is? Observe, listen, and *don't* ask questions. Unfortunately, some parents are lost when it comes to understanding how to do each of these.

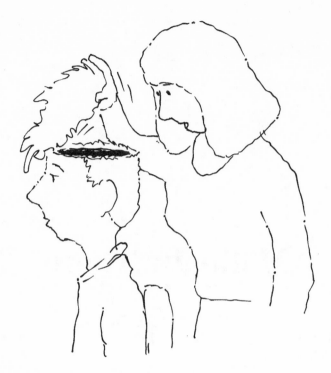

Observe. See if you can figure out who your teen is by quietly observing how he behaves, what she likes and dislikes. Try to pick up on subtle signals. Look into your teen's face. Notice if the expression has shifted from rested to tired, or from solid to vulnerable. Look at the way she moves, the position of his shoulders, the presence or absence of a bounce in the walk. Observe her emotions. Is she sad, glad, or mad? Is she holding in these feelings? Is fear present? Is he hopeful or doubtful, content or confused? If you look, you can catch these "places"—emotional, physical, and social—that your teen inhabits.

Listen. See if you can just listen—with no judgments or opinions about anything. If you're not listening, you'll seem incredibly phoney to a teen, and they can detect it instantly. They'll also tend to tune you out when *you* have something to express. So show interest. Encourage your teen to be herself and talk about what she loves. Make your teen feel comfortable, so she will open up. Your most important togethering tool is listening deeply! Know that you have a lot of listening to do.

Stop the questions. See if you can carry on a conversation without asking one question. One mother confessed: "I do the stupid parent thing. I ask questions, and I don't even know how to do it differently." How do you have a conversation without questions? Teens are good at it! Be a fly on the wall and listen to their technique. You will discover that they don't ask each other any questions. They just talk. They would feel free to say "Gosh, I hate Ms. Duff (a coach)." "Man, what a jerk." "This is what I heard she did to somebody else." They would keep talking about it. But a parent would say, "What happened?"

Catch yourself the next time you ask your son's or daughter's friends all your usual questions. They will like you a whole lot better! We send a lot of signals when we ask questions. We let them know what we think is important by the questions we ask. How obvious this is to a teen! Listen to these typical parent questions, and I'm sure you will recognize some of your own: "How are your classes going this semester?" "Do you have a part-time job?" "Did your field hockey team win their last game?" "What are you going to do over spring break?" "Do you like your teachers this term?" "What are your plans for the summer?" "So, what college are you applying to?" "Why do you like that college?" Remind yourself, again and again if necessary, to stop asking so many questions.

Teens find our questions annoying. It is one sure way for your teen to tune you out. They don't want to give you too much information because it feels like you are prying too much into their lives. Try to spark your teen's interest in a conversation instead. Say, "I had an awesome day—I took a nap, did some reading, and called some close friends." Or try, "You wouldn't believe what I did this evening, or who I saw today." Then let your teen respond to you. If he doesn't feel like talking, let it be. Remember: if you ask questions, I guarantee, your teen will give you a zero- to three-word answer, then hurry away from you.

A mother shared with me how well she got to know her teen's "inside" by observing, listening, and not asking questions. The topic was why did he dress "that way" (i.e., with an orange mohawk and clothes that had holes in them). She said: "I think you dress the way you do to express yourself differently—that you really want to tell the world that you are different from kids who dress at Lands' End. I think it also helps you find friends who have similar interests." Her teen was completely taken aback because she was exactly right. But then her teen added something else to the conversation. He said, "Another reason I dress this way is that if out of 100 people, 99 won't speak to me because I have a mohawk and my clothes have holes, then the one person who speaks to me will become a true friend because that person speaks to me regardless of how I look and that person is interested in who I am." And that's key with teens. They want to be accepted and regarded for who they are inside.

If you want to discover who your teen really is,
observe, listen, and don't ask questions.

13

Tips for
Talking to Teens

One exasperated parent I interviewed told me that if you really want to have a conversation with a teen, you should be in the car for a very long trip because they will actually talk to you. (That is, if they don't happen to have a walkman with them, which is just unlucky. She actually suggested sneaking dead batteries into their walkman when they weren't looking.) If you don't have such a trip planned, let me suggest some talking tips.

Be available. The first step in communicating with your teen is to make yourself available. Let your teen choose the time. (For those of you who plan professional meetings well in advance of events, and work with calendars to make schedules happen, this

may require quite an adjustment on your part.) As long as they know you are there for them, they will come. There may be no advance warning when your teen arrives, plops down, and is ready to open up. Seize this opportunity. Often it's late at night. Maybe just when you're ready to go to bed. (This is one of our teen's regular talk times.) Whatever you do, try to be there. Timing is everything with your teen.

Tackle issues quickly. When issues come up, talk them through. Don't avoid them. This is important. If you find yourself unable to get your teen to sit down and talk, try the following technique. The person who says, "I can't talk right now" has to come back thirty minutes later; or if not thirty minutes, then one hour later, or two hours later. An agreement is reached as to when. The responsibility for bringing the conversation together at the agreed upon time falls on the person who was unavailable. This way, no one plays the role of the avoider.

Be open and direct. Go easy on the unsolicited advice. Put everything on the table, even be confrontational, if necessary.

Don't let anything prevent you from talking openly together. The style of talking that is best is direct, straight, and clear. Don't give advice unless your teen asks for it. My own teenage son said to me recently: "What I really want from you is for you to express your feelings. I want to hear what your feelings are." So I've been doing this recently, and it works out a lot better. For example, I'll share my feelings about this academic class or that school, or my feelings about a teacher, or just anything. I always held them back before, because I didn't want to influence him so he could discover how he thought about it. But now he wants us to share what we think. He has even asked us to do this at the dinner table. (He doesn't want us to talk about the events of the day anymore, which I think ends up with us asking him lots of questions, but instead to express our own feelings more.)

Look for the good and acknowledge what you see. In our fast-paced world, it's easy for teens and adults alike to lose touch with their unique gifts and talents. Reminding teens of the special beauty within them can light up their path and encourage them to take their next steps, whatever they may be.

Here's how our family put this idea into practice: During a special dinner on a family summer vacation, my husband asked us each to identify our number-one talent. Our son James then suggested that we expand this "self-study" by having every family member add what they think that person's key talent is. It worked best when each person shared their own answer first, followed by the other member's thoughts. (An added benefit to us, as parents, was discovering what each of our children saw as *our* key attributes. One is always surprised by these perceptions. I strongly encourage you to do this activity for this reason alone.)

Thomas, at ten, said his greatest talent was that he was good at basketball. Others added: getting along and talking with people of all ages; blending into all kinds of groups, young and old; making us smile when we look at him, even when we are in the worst mood; clearing things up right away so no obstacles get in his way; and always persevering to learn and understand something. James, at almost fifteen, said his greatest talent was to be able to identify what other people want to hear. (He said that this enables him to usually get what he wants!) Others added: drawing and painting; seeing beauty in things; having a sharp and precise business mind; and being decisive, having excellent judgment and taking important details into consideration. John, at sixteen and a half, said his greatest talent was being able to recognize love and see it in other people. (He said he didn't care if somebody was "cool" or had nice clothes; his "screen" was whether a person was kind and nice inside.) Others added: using his eyes to see things and then translate what he saw into knowledge; being intuitive and perceptive with people; sensing; and last of all, jogging.

Encourage teens to take time to appreciate their inner strengths as well as those of the people around them. It can light up the journey ahead for all concerned.

In talking with your teen, try these tips: be available, tackle issues quickly, be open and direct, go easy on the unsolicited advice, and finally, look for the good and acknowledge what you see.

14

⊠

Letting
Feelings Out

Teens, like adults, are entitled to their feelings. When a teen is angry, sad, or otherwise upset, don't deny, rationalize, or try to "fix" the feeling. Responses like "Don't be angry" or "That shouldn't hurt" or "Try not to be sad" are so common that, at first, they sound correct. But this is far from true. What your teen really needs is for you to validate the feeling. Validation requires a parent to: (1) listen and try to understand the feeling, (2) acknowledge that it exists—mirroring it back, if necessary, and finally (3) accept rather than try to alter it. Do this as much as you can, as often as you can. Validation sounds something like this: "I understand why you're upset about your grades, when you studied so

long and hard" or "It's OK to feel the way you do about your friend, Robert. You've spent a lot of time with him, more time than the other kids, and you may have a more accurate read on him because of this."

As a rule of thumb, try to allow your teen to express *any* emotion to you. Even give her room to be messy with her emotions. If she has kept a lid on her feelings, she may have strong anger for another teen, a teacher, a group, or her school. She may agonize over her own decisions, wondering "Why did I join the swim team?" or "What was I thinking when I decided to take that difficult after-school class?" An assignment may be unclear or frustrating, she may not feel good, or she may be concerned that her boyfriend's friends don't like her. Give her room to express all this "stuff"—however irrational, explosive, or volatile. Let her get it out. When teens learn to verbalize their powerful, strong, even "dangerous" emotions in safe, appropriate ways, they are less likely to feel compelled to act them out.

Teens often need help in learning how to put these feelings into words. Show them, through your own example, how this is done. Never forget the very important role that *you* play in teaching them how to communicate emotion. Teens are watching and listening to you at all times (although they may not want you to think so). You are their *role model*. Take advantage of this opportunity. Don't hide your own feelings. Express them in words. Do this often. Try to get good at it. Once you establish the habit, it gets easier. For now, practice. For instance, if someone (your teen perhaps?) is treating you badly, explain how this makes you feel. Say: "I feel angry when you say crummy things about my friends" or "I am sad to see you so upset about that" or "I felt hurt when you yelled at me like that" or "I know you're going through some tough stuff, but when you treat me that way, I don't feel like being around you." Show teens how to unveil their emotions by letting your own feelings out. It'll be good for you too!

Encourage teens to share their feelings with you—
then validate them. Through your own example, demonstrate
how to express emotions safely and effectively.

15

The Judge
and the Detective

"I'm stupid because I don't have a girlfriend." "I'm a dork and can't talk to girls." "I am a fake because I'm always smiling and happy." "I suck in acting class." "I look stupid because I am nervous and can't look calm." "I stink at soccer because I can't trap the ball today." "I can't keep my own opinions around Bob because his opinions are so strong." "I'm not very smart in science because I didn't do well on my exam." All of these self-demeaning thoughts originate from an intruder called "the Judge." He is the inner critic, the mastermind of negative feelings and low self-esteem. While the Judge lives inside everyone, he especially likes to take charge during the teen years.

How can the Judge be so effective? He uses a strategy called "partial validity." Here is how it works: After missing a shot, the Judge says to the young player, "You suck at basketball." This is partially true because he did miss a shot (even though everybody misses some shots), but now the player thinks he's terrible at basketball. Masterfully, the Judge always backs up the insults with partially true facts. Most of the time, these facts are insignificant—like missing one goal, doing poorly on one area of a test, or bombing on one quiz.

Stealth is a critical part of his strategy. To most all teens, the Judge's involvement in their lives is imperceptible. Whispering slyly within their minds, he criticizes every move and turn. The Judge especially likes to pop up and be critical when a teen is involved in something important—like going out on a big date, making a difficult speech in a forensics debate, or racing against a fast jogger in a track meet.

Dr. John Cooper, a clinical psychologist for almost forty years, was an expert on the Judge. Before his unexpected death several years ago, he shared with me his insights on how the Judge maneuvers inside the heads of teens. According to Dr. Cooper, between the ages of twelve and nineteen, biological and chemical changes are bombarding a teen's brain. Feelings of confusion, isolation, embarrassment, and a host of other emotions make teens feel out of control—as if they're barely hanging on to their insides. Stress builds up and control wanes, setting up a teen for internal self-indictments and criticisms. An avalanche of anxiety manifests both during the day and in sleep at night. (You may want to ask your teen how he is sleeping. I suspect "peacefully" is not the answer you'll hear.) Unfortunately, until the biological, chemical, and emotional chaos subsides—at around sixteen or seventeen years of age—confusion, self-doubt, and anxiety run rampant in the teenage psyche. The Judge is sneaky, clever at his craft—and he takes full advantage of your teen's inner turmoil and vulnerability.

What is the best way to work around the Judge? First, stay alert to his sneaky strategy—to harbor partially valid evidence against your teen and put a negative spin on it. You might also try using a "Judge Book" to catch him in the act. This technique helps disprove the Judge's insults and prevents him from playing such a major role in shaping your teen's self-image. Get a blank notebook for your teen. When she feels bad or uncomfortable about herself, encourage her to think about why she has this feeling. Try to expose the Judge's accusations (e.g., "you suck at dance class") and write them down. Give it time to simmer, and then go back after a day. Have your teen put on her Detective hat and search for the pieces to the puzzle—break down each one of the Judge's insults, dissect its partial truth, and observe its irrational and inaccurate nature. Let's look closely at the three Judge book entries that follow.

Judge: "You're a dork because you went to dinner with your parents" (entry #1 in book)
Ask the Judge what he means by "dork" The Judge gives you other general statements . . . like "loser" and "fool" and "loner."

Detective: There is no supportive evidence for me being a "dork" because I go out to dinner with my parents. I know there is nothing wrong with going to dinner with them. Everyone goes to dinner with their family.

Judge: But if your friends see you, they'll think you're a dork.

Detective: The truth is that if other teens see me, then they are probably eating dinner with their parents too. Even if they're not, it's still totally normal to eat dinner with my family.

Judge: "You suck at baseball." (entry #2 in book)
Ask the Judge why you suck at baseball, or to define the word "suck." The Judge says it means striking out or not catching the fly ball.

Detective: Everybody swings at the wrong time or misses balls—even the players who've been at it for a long time. It's completely normal, and I am still good at baseball, even though I make some errors too. It's part of playing the game.

Judge: "You look stupid in those clothes." (entry #3 in book)
> Ask the Judge to define "stupid." The Judge says it means "different."

Detective: Everyone looks different, is born different, and is supposed to be different. It is completely normal to look different. In fact, different is good.

A teenage brain is going through massive changes, chemical imbalances, and enormous shifts. The resulting chaos provides the Judge with fertile ground in which to plant accusations and self-demeaning thoughts. When a teen feels bad about herself, know that the Judge is sitting high on her shoulders. Helping your teen to confront her internal Judge head-on will go a long way to ensure that she keeps *her* head on—straight, that is.

*When it comes to the Judge, a little work with the
Detective can restore a teen's perspective.*

16

Buried Treasure

One way to stop the Judge before he insults your teen is to help him uncover his inner "buried treasure"—his self-esteem. This is one of the most important things we can do. One way for your teen to find his buried treasure is to identify his strengths. Unfortunately, they are often concealed. Use affirmations to bring them to light. (These are positive statements about our strengths—strengths we already have, as well as those we would like to develop.) Have your teen write a list of affirmations and post them in a special place where he will see them every day. Below are some examples of one teen's affirmations.

I am completely positive that

1. I am awesome at golf, basketball, roller blading, ice-skating, jogging, and baseball.
2. I love to have fun and am open to other's ideas, experiences, and suggestions.
3. I am enthusiastic, kind, understanding, loyal, and honest.
4. I love sharing love and complimenting others.
5. I am a great teacher and mentor; I love doing it.
6. I am intelligent in social studies, math, English, science, and French.
7. I am determined, disciplined, and focused.
8. I am funny, spontaneous, exuberant, and love laughter.
9. I am extremely perceptive and intuitive, and I can read and understand people. I use this in my kindness.
10. I love to PARTY! and have a great time.

When teens can identify positive things about themselves, their self-worth grows. And feeling good about who you are is the foundation for all other learning.

Self-reliance develops inside the teen as she learns to see her beauty from her own vantage point. Learn to praise your teen in a way that encourages her to acknowledge her own strengths, from her own point of view. Instead of "*I'm* proud of you" or "*I* think you did a nice job on your Spanish test," try "*You* must be pleased with yourself for studying your Spanish so hard and doing so well on your assignment." Over time, praise of this kind will place the teen in front of her own mirror, where she can acknowledge herself for her own strengths and achievements. When a teen knows her resources and can say positive things about herself, she has discovered her buried treasure.

One of my teenage sons, for example, has recently recognized his achievement in running. We live in the city, and there are frequent 5 kilometer races on weekends that are open to any person upon simply registering. The first time he ran a 5K, his time was 29 minutes and 18 seconds. The next weekend, he ran it in 28 minutes and 28 seconds. When he came across the finish line on his third 5K race, his time was 24 minutes and 12 seconds. He said to me several days after that race, "I can't believe how well I did—my first mile was in 7 minutes and 35 seconds, the second mile was in 7 minutes and 37 seconds, and the last 1.1 mile was in 9 minutes flat" (5 kilometers = 3.1 miles). He was pleased with his own achievement and could say positive things about himself, aware of his own inner resources. He now builds his own self-esteem—and daily adds to his inner treasure chest.

Self-reliant teens can identify their strengths
and list their resources.

PART 3

Exploring

17

Surfing Life

Our son John was thirteen when he first became interested in surfing. While the sport itself is challenging and physically demanding, what has struck me most is the time and emphasis placed on looking for just the right waves. In search of suitable waves, we routinely get in our car and drive to the nearest beach to "check them out." A good wave has the following characteristics: It must be powerful, but not vertical. This means that the "lip" or "pocket" of the wave (the observable wave edge that the surfer rides) must be curved and smooth. You want it to break along the beach and have a roll to it, and not "dump" all the water at the same time. The wave should be smooth like glass, not choppy. And finally, it should have a continuous motion, as though an un-

derwater engine is keeping it powered up and moving along, so it won't die out too quickly.

   If the waves at the first beach don't have a number of these characteristics, we drive farther down the coast, to the next beach. Then I pull off the road while John looks out the car window or jumps out to get a closer look. This search can go on for several hours. On one occasion, when the waves weren't good anywhere (after eight beaches were "analyzed"), we turned around and headed home. Most of the time, however, John finally settles on a beach, sometimes requiring us to return to one of the places that we've already checked out. (This tells us that he is deciding in favor of less-than-perfect waves, because he *really* wants to go surfing.)

   My three sons and I have learned to really love this whole

process of getting in the car, driving to the different beaches (usually to the tunes of the "Beach Boys") and checking out the waves. When you head out to surf, you *never know* what the waves will be like. One surfer's rule of thumb is that you can never expect to return to the same beach two days in a row and find similarly good wave conditions. So if the waves aren't especially good for surfing, we play in the sand, look for shells and colored glass, or walk along the beach, where we are quietly reminded that one never knows what lies ahead. In this way, on any given day, whether we watch John ride the biggest waves or simply catch a glimpse of the ocean, the trip brings us to a place that we treasure. Being there together is what it's all about.

Things don't always go as expected, or as we would like
them to ideally, but we can make the best of whatever
we find and make the most of our time together.

18

Rude and Cantankerous

Among the parents I interviewed for this book, the oft-repeated consensus was "I can't believe how rude my teen can be!" One parent said to me: "Even your kid is rude? That gives me great hope. Would you mention that in your book? It helps to know that your teen is rude, too. My husband didn't believe it. He didn't believe that anybody else's kid could be that rude!" Another parent confided: "I actually don't want him living in the house anymore because he really isn't fun to be around." Another said, "I just want back the nice person that used to live with us."

When I interviewed parents about their teens, at the end of our sessions we'd brainstorm book titles. A few of my favorites were:

- I'M NOT KEEPING A JOURNAL BECAUSE I DON'T WANT TO REMEMBER ANY OF IT!
- I WANT TO TRADE MY TEEN IN FOR SOMEONE ELSE'S
- I DON'T WANT HIM AROUND ANYMORE—-HE ISN'T FUN!
- FAMILY WRECKERS

In our interview setting, parents revealed their enormous frustrations with their teens. They seemed greatly relieved to share them with someone else—and to learn that other parents were struggling to come to terms with the rude and cantankerous teenagers in *their* families. One mother summed it up this way: "It's really important to be in close touch with other parents to find out that their teens are as awful as yours."

So when your teen is overpowering, compare notes with other parents on how they are coping with their home turbulence. The following are some ideas I gleaned from other parents in the course of writing this book. One parent shared the tactic she uses when her daughter starts arguing: "I say, 'Oh, I know what you're doing. You're doing that teenage arguing thing. I'm not playing.' Then I don't talk anymore and it drives her nuts." This mother reduced conflict and tension on the home front by simply stepping out of the combative dialogue with her daughter. Know that non-involvement can be an effective response, and use it more often.

One father I know said that the best bit of parenting he ever did was to invest in a good paint-ball gun and join his son in combative, spirited play. After an entire day spent hunting down and shooting one another, they experienced a rare sense of calm, peaceful serenity. On one occasion the boy's mother joined in too. She actually "took out" one of the "best guys" at the paint-ball range and became something of a legend there. Both parents noted a tremendously increased level of respect and connection with their son. Try to find ways to step into your teen's world.

So try these helpful hints from those parents that I interviewed:

1. Compare notes with other parents.
2. Try nonparticipation in quarrels.
3. Take a step into their world.

Finally, it's important to know that this is only a stage. As one parent put it, "However your teen is being right now, it's not how he's going to be for the rest of his life."

Know that you aren't alone in trying to cope with a rude, cantankerous teen. Try to meet with other parents for support and an exchange of ideas whenever you can.

19

Fending
for Themselves

Several months ago, one of my own teenage sons said to me, "I don't want you to be supportive." I didn't get it—and it took me about six weeks to finally figure it out. That's a long time when you're in the midst of trying to learn the right moves with your teen, so I'm going to share my discovery with you. Here it is: Teens love to do it all on their own. This is true in most every area where we want to offer our help. One mother shared with me the following story.

> "My son found a job on his own at Starbucks, and he is so proud of himself. He's going into computers some day. I think it is silly that he's not looking for a job in computers. There

are computer jobs everywhere. I found a little software company right around the corner from where we live. I stopped by
there one day and asked if their boss ever hired anybody, and
they said 'Sure, he might.' I gave the information to my son,
but he wouldn't have anything to do with it."

My own son went out job hunting and was turned down at three
restaurants in the area where we live. He said to me shortly after
his search, "It's really hard to get a job, isn't it?" This was a valuable discovery for him. I can't think of a better piece of life learning than this. He now knows just how difficult it is to find any
job—let alone the right job. Had I gotten involved in the job-hunt-
ing expedition myself, he might have gotten one, but would not
have learned this golden nugget. Teens don't want much from us.
As another mother discovered,

> "Teenagers don't want much, so tread carefully . . . They'd
> rather miss the opportunity to apply for a summer job than
> know that you found one for them. 'If I need a job, I'll get my
> own.' And I'm thinking, 'But I have all these resources. I know
> people. I can help you. I can make these things happen!' And
> the more you make happen for them, the more they don't like
> you for it. That's really tough. So back off."

Teens have an overwhelming desire not to depend on us.
Less is more. Try less involvement in their lives. (You can even try
doing *nothing*. See what happens and learn from it!) This is difficult and troublesome for most parents because it denies us our
importance—something all parents, including myself, like to think
we have. One mother offers her retrospective: "I wish I'd done a
lot less. Just let them be, without being all over them every
minute." If you are a parent who has done everything for your

child-turned-teen, now is the perfect time to stop. It's never too late. Be guided by the fact that teens want to fend for themselves—more than just about anything else.

Teens want to do it themselves. Let them!

20

Gunny Sacks

Gunny sacks were placed over our heads. In the dark of a Colorado night, the four of us were driven for several hours in the back of a pickup truck to an unknown place. We were then dumped in the middle of this "somewhere" with just enough food for three days, plus a few maps to help us find our way back to the base camp in three days. It was the final expedition of our Outward Bound group. I was nineteen.

When morning came, we made a lot of decisions. After studying the nearby mountains, we guessed at our location, took a tentative bearing on a uniquely shaped peak, and mapped out a possible return path "home," praying we had been accurate in charting our course. We had a very long way to go to get back.

Conflict served as a teacher. Within our group of four, disagreement surfaced early on. Sam and Rich were competitive and

fast. They wanted to be the first to return to base camp. Beating the other small expedition groups that had been dumped off in other locations in the region was important to them. But Paul and I felt that the area was too spectacular to rush through. We wanted to soak in the rare, untouched beauty of our surroundings and take the full three days to return. Still, the other two kept pushing and hurrying relentlessly along every path. After a day and a half of bickering, we finally split up.

To my dismay, Paul's leg gave out in a grove of aspen trees. He couldn't walk, and I knew I had to perform the emergency procedure I had learned several weeks earlier at the beginning of the course. I marked Paul's location along the trail, so that I could locate him upon my return, then I headed out to find our base camp or a telephone to call for medical help. I was entirely on my own. When I heard the unlikely sound of a motorbike, my rescue strategy became clear and much easier than I had first thought. I hitched a ride from the biker, who took me to where I could make a rescue call. When Paul was "saved," we returned to base camp in shortly under two day's time from the outset.

The expedition had been difficult and intense. There was competition, dissension, and compromise along the way. We learned to keep our eyes open, test our limits, and push beyond those limits to do seemingly impossible things. We worked through the conflict, decision-making, and trust issues that surfaced, and grew, individually and together—and sometimes apart.

So it is with most teens. Suddenly—after years of cruising along in the comfort of family and friends—they find themselves lost in a dark, unknown "somewhere": the place where childhood and adult worlds merge. Feeling confused and disoriented, they must somehow find their way through.

As in our Outward Bound journey, group qualities of togetherness, connection, and trust need to be balanced with individual experiences of personal growth and solitude. Teens will be forced to deal with crises and conflict. At times, they will need to split from a group, join another, or try a new path of their own. We parents can give them compasses and maps and teach them how to use these tools, but ultimately, teens must set their own courses and seek whatever destiny is to be theirs.

Help teens learn the tools to chart their own life course,
so they can begin to find their way—if they should
ever find themselves "lost in the dark."

21

Freedom

Freedom is the ability to choose and the power to act. Too often, we snatch away valuable learning experiences by choosing and acting for our teenagers. But don't forget, the skill to choose and the power to act must be nurtured and taught. One of my sons put it like this:

> I need to do some things on my own, planning stuff, making decisions. I'm not asking you to change, but to just let me do that—to make my own decisions, to make may own plans, to decide on my own life. I don't want you to worry about me getting good grades, or not focusing on my studies. If you give me this freedom of my own decisions, I feel, and know, that I will be able to do school work, extra curricular activities, talk with friends, and everything with more focus and dynamic

creativity than anyone, or even I, thought possible because I'll be so much happier doing it. I don't want you guys to completely avoid my decision-making or have things become awkward between us when I need to make a decision. I really want your input, I just want to be able to make my own decisions . . . . For me to even *begin* to establish *my* own set of values and beliefs and morals, I need the freedom from you to do so.

We parents hold the keys to the door of independence. If we let a teen open that door, she will see glimpses of different realities. Seeing these other vistas, a teen can learn to choose what she thinks is best for her, and then act on that choice.

Let me take an example on our home front. The teenage son quoted above wanted to change high schools—two months into his junior year. He had undergone lots of change over the summer before his junior year and decided he wanted to check out another view when school began in the fall. He wanted to leave the small private school he had attended for the last two years and move to a large public school. We went along with his decision and stayed in communication about our support. He knew we were his allies—behind him, whatever he chose to do.

We witnessed him starting over, trying to make new friends, and getting acquainted with a completely different school culture. Letting him follow his own path, we looked on as he experienced more bad days than good ones. But he became stronger and wiser. If we had told him to stay put and stick it out in his "old" school, he would have missed this life-changing lesson, which he identified as follows: "While I'm sure I'll continue to undergo many changes as I grow, I've learned that change occurs internally. You don't have to change your external environment to allow changes to be made within you." Freedom can teach and change—even alter the course of a life. Be sure to let your teen experience it now under your tutelage.

Give your teen the freedom to choose and
the power to act, and support his decisions,
even when they are life-altering.

22

Nourishing Mistakes and Hard-Won Lessons

Winston Churchill once said, "I've eaten many of my words, and I've found them nourishing." Do you support your teen's effort to find out who she is, try things on her own, and make her own "nourishing" mistakes? Often, a parent's role is to simply watch the development. Freedom is the starting point. If a parent gives a teen the freedom to make decisions and experience her stumbles, she will learn.

Switching schools during an extremely turbulent, transformative time in his life led my son to many discoveries and lessons. He experienced bureaucratic school settings for the first time; discovered the value of active, rather than passive, learning (classroom

settings were more teacher-dominated at his new school); and learned that teaching, at its very best, has passion and caring. (I think it's fair to say he learned all of this the hard way.)

When our son wanted to go back to his old high school, after experiencing the new one for six months, he learned that he couldn't return as quickly as he had left. It wouldn't be fair to both teachers and students at his old school, who would have to play catch-up and make exceptions for him not completing all his missed work. Lesson learned: You can't always "unmake" a decision as quickly as you made it the first time.

He also learned that one doesn't get to have everything one

wants; that institutions, including schools, don't change rapidly; and that rapid-fire changes he initiates affect the people around him. Social repercussions occur. He saw that when he makes a wild card move like he did, it not only impacts him but also his family, friendships, teachers and school—the social circles and structures—around him, and he has to noodle through all the change and regain control in his own life. While he had the guts to be really different and to make change happen, he learned that his move affected many others.

The final lesson he learned, my son summed up as follows: "My junior year, I switched high schools by my own choice. I wanted more diversity, more individuation, and generally more freedom to study on my own . . . connect ideas in my own way. I found out that 'true' freedom exists only when it has boundaries, organization, and discipline." As difficult as it was to watch his painful change process, I learned this key parent lesson: "I don't care what you decide—I just want you to do what *you* want." While it may sound obvious and easy to do, it isn't. The teen years are about your teen making choices and learning from mistakes along the way.

When parents let their teens experience mistakes,
they discover, learn, and are "nourished"
through hard-won lessons.

23

Primer on Drugs

Here are the names of the popular drugs in our area at the time of this writing: "Ecstasy," "Roofies," "Liquid X," "Special K." The names don't sound very troublesome. But watch out for them. They're dangerous. Some young people aren't even aware they're taking them. *Esctasy,* or "e," is a mind-altering drug with hallucinogenic and stimulant effects; teens dance all night with it. It causes heatstroke and dehydration among new users who don't drink sufficient water. *Roofies* are potent sleeping pills with euphoric effects; they are called the "date rape drug" because many women aren't sure whether they were raped or not—because they have no memory. *Liquid X* can be slipped into drinks; users are knocked out and have no memory. It can cause coma and death. *Special K* (ketamine) has similar effects to LSD, including hallucinations, delirium, confusion, and irrational behavior; it is marketed as an anesthetic for human and veterinary use.

Share the following precautions with your teen to protect him or her from ingesting drugs unknowingly.

- Be especially cautious of new dates.
- Buy your own drinks and watch as they are delivered to your table.
- Unattended drinks should be dumped.
- Don't drink from communal punch bowls at parties.
- Have safer parties by telling kids to bring their own drinks, open the cans themselves, and, after setting down drinks (even briefly) to avoid drinking from them again.

How do you keep your teen away from drugs? Here's the game (excuse the pun) plan: Support recreational activities that have absolutely no hint of drugs. Consider the following examples. One family with two teens launched a new community service agency, based on their love for animals. It's called PAWS (Pets Are Worth Saving). They arrange for the adoption of unwanted cats and dogs, to prevent the animals from being destroyed.

A group of teens I know started running together with their grade school coach, and entered 5 and 10K races during the summer. The following summer, all five of us entered these same races as a family. I now greatly look forward to these weekend races. They offer recreation that is fun, people-oriented, sponsored by a civic cause and usually take place in a beautiful setting on the lake front. Awards are given too—and teens love to receive ribbons and medals for their physical efforts.

Recreation, for one of my teenage sons, has involved learning swing dancing and the Lindy Hop (a jitterbug dance that originated in Harlem). He started swing lessons two years ago, and now dances in a teen dance group called Jeepers Creepers. Besides competing nationally, they put on performances in Chicago for different audiences. Practice is time-consuming. There isn't much time left for other activities outside school. (If he adds one school sport to this extracurricular mix, his free time is booked to the max.) My son must be in shape to rigorously dance for several hours straight. Physically, it would be difficult to use drugs (or alcohol for that matter), stay in tune with the complex steps required, and keep together with a dancing partner. This form of recreation doesn't fit with drugs.

So look for engaging forms of recreation with your teen. If sports don't match their interests, try dance, guitar lessons, karate, drama, art, cooking classes, or an adventuresome outdoor wilderness program. Let your teen pick from the assortment of choices out there. You'll be surprised at how many different opportunities there are.

Don't forget that teens are struggling, pressured, and often confused. Something unsettling always seems to be going on in a teen's immediate life. Close friends and school success can act as an antidote, and bring security and comfort to a teen. One eighteen-year-old Ecstasy user, said that "e" allowed her to get closer to people, be at ease with herself, and right with the world. To keep teens off drugs, this is exactly where focus must be placed. So, encourage your teen to develop intimate friendships, feel good about and discover her strengths (see "Buried Treasure" chapter),

and be successful with her "work"—both school and outside, or recreational, activities.

And finally, to become more informed and aware of drugs, it's helpful to establish a network among parents to educate one another and share information. There are a lot of drugs that are easily available. Know that their risks are usually grossly underestimated. Parents can learn about this misinformation, and get the accurate word out to their teens and other families. Read all the drug pamphlets you can. Keep your ear to the ground to learn what's out there for teens to grab. And help teens focus on friends, school, and extracurricular activities instead.

Become acutely aware of what popular drugs are
available in your area, share precautions with your teen,
and encourage recreational activities that are
fun, people-oriented, and positive.

24

Ground Rules

Family systems can be closed or open when it comes to ground rules. In a closed system, teens are given orders, threats, and warnings by their parents. In a totally open family, teens are allowed to do what they want, and parents often throw up their hands when the going gets tough. The first approach puts teens on a short leash, while the second puts them on one that is too long. Of course, the ideal system is somewhere in between—structured enough to promote healthy boundaries, yet flexible enough to allow for growth and exploration. There needs to be a balance between structure and flexibility. Teens need enough direction and control to guide them, yet enough room to let them breathe, learn, and discover.

We want to nurture creative, independent adults, but also cre-

ate a family culture where everyone is respected. Setting and maintaining appropriate boundaries helps to protect each family member's dignity (and sanity!) and to preserve reasonable harmony in your home. Delineate these boundaries by (1) setting rules and guidelines, (2) communicating and reinforcing rules, (3) executing consequences for broken rules, and (4) upping the ante for serious or repeat offenses.

Set ground rules in place. If you haven't done so already, put some practical boundaries or parameters in place. These are the basic behaviors required by teens. Here are some that we adopted on our home front.

GROUND RULES:

1. Interact and communicate with each family member (brothers in particular) with genuine compassion and kindness.
2. Complete high school and get passing grades. (If a teen is college-bound, parents may want to keep a higher standard.)

3. Check in nightly.

4. No drinking, smoking, drugs, or any other illegal activities.

5. Eat, sleep, exercise, and keep clothes clean—-so we know these basics are covered.

6. Do assigned chores at home.

7. Be available to help in case of family emergencies.

Know that teens hate fixed, out-of-date, and inhuman rules with a passion. (Have you noticed?) They want to be involved in the process of establishing them. So sit down with your teens and work together on a list of specific rules for your household. Give them the opportunity to come up with ideas, add to the list, and comment on anything related to each of the rules. Also consider special times where your teen needs an exception to a rule—a friend is moving away, a once-a-year dance is held, a final event is celebrated (e.g., graduation, end of swim team). And as teens become older, don't forget to accommodate their eagerness to stay out later. The goal is to arrive at a mutually generated and agreed upon set of rules, but one that leaves the door open for adjusting them a bit down the road. Teens want the freedom to change the rules, so listen to their input, and be open to revising the rules as it makes sense to you to do so.

Communicate and reinforce rules. Teens need limits and boundaries; they need also to hear the word "no!" and the reasons why they can't do something. Try to give clear, straight answers. Be calm and firm, but hold to your point of view. For example, say "Under no circumstances can driving occur while drinking." Or, "It is imperative that we know where you are at night in case we have to reach you, so give us detailed information when you check in."

Be sure your teen knows the rules. Use formal communication devices like bulletin boards or postings on the refrigerator door to keep guidelines clear in everyone's mind. Reinforce with informal "reminders" as you feel they are needed like: "If you forget to do your chores, we all suffer."

Execute consequences of broken rules. Your teen will be more likely to learn something about himself if he has input, than if the consequences for broken rules are handed down from above. So work with your teen to find agreement on the consequences of breaking the rules—and breaking them repeatedly too. If agreement can't be reached, negotiate, or even try what your teen wants. I'm always willing to go along with a teen's request, or at least give it a try, if it sounds even remotely workable. I'm happy to err on the side of taking a little risk—to teach something or to allow for an even greater good.

So what do you do when rules are broken? The consequences should match the "criticality" of the rule. Rules go into different buckets—different categories. Rules involving safety, legality, threats to health, or harm to others (e.g., drinking and driving) have different consequences than rules that are good for you or your family (e.g., doing your house chores). If your teen doesn't do his chores, try talk first, like—"You don't get it. As a member of our family, your help and involvement are greatly needed. If you forget to take out the garbage, it's sitting around for one more week." (For more serious offenses, you may need to bring in a consequence right away. See below.)

Up the ante. After talk and explanation have been exhausted, if your teen still doesn't keep the rule, then you must up the ante. Remove allowance, time with friends, or anything else that has great importance in their lives. If your teen drinks while driving, the consequence is to take away car privileges. Above anything else, your teen must know where the boundaries lie.

Let's take the example of curfews and explore how to set, maintain, and execute the consequences of broken rules.

SETTING RULES: Involve your teen in setting her nighttime boundaries. At fourteen, you may want her home at 11:00 p.m. She wants 11:30. Reach a middle point and agree on it—say 11:15. Or if she has good reasons for 11:30, go with it. You don't always have to be the "winner." (A friend's "curfew time" always enters into the picture. It is fine to not consider it, unless this becomes a compelling reason for your teen's viewpoint. Then you should.) As your teen gets older, the arrival hour is negotiated toward an increasingly later time. For example, at sixteen, it may be 12:30 a.m. The important point is that you reach an agreement together as to this time.

COMMUNICATING AND REINFORCING RULES: Be sure your teen is clear about when you expect him or her home. Post the agreed-upon time on the refrigerator with colorful magnets for all to see. Reinforce with a verbal reminder like: "Look forward to seeing you around midnight!"

EXECUTING CONSEQUENCES OF BROKEN RULES: When she is late, give her the freedom and opportunity to comment and explain. Maybe unplanned events occurred, like a flat tire, or a surprise party for your teen, causing an unpredictable delay. See if you can find a solution to the problem together. Keep your discussion open. Ask her what she feels should be done. It's worth exploring a teen's "solution." I like going with a teen's idea for a first infraction of the rule. It puts the responsibility back in their court. It also communicates that you are willing to let them have one more try at their request, before moving to the next more serious step.

UP THE ANTE: If a teen still breaks the curfew rule, let the agreed-upon consequences fall into place because talking was ineffective. Since you and your teen have already discussed these consequences, you are not forced into the position of playing the "heavy." The consequence we set up with our teens for curfew violations is one that our teens chose: If they fail to call and let us know where they are (in case we need to reach them) and the time they will be home, then they have to stay home next time they want to go out. Other parents I know do the following: ground a teen to the home front; take away car keys; or remove home privileges, including TV, computer, and telephone use. If your teen has missed curfew because drinking or drugs were involved, then the consequences are more serious. Simply enact the consequences that you and your teen agreed upon when setting up the rule. You'll find that you don't need to be heavy handed but can do so lovingly, even kidding some.

Set reasonable boundaries to protect your family culture.
Give your teen a key role in setting the boundaries;
communicate clearly what the boundaries are, through
written and verbal reinforcements; execute the consequences
of broken rules—and up the ante when necessary.

PART 4

Acquiring Skills

25

A Boat
on the Water

Several years ago, my husband and I took our three young sons fishing. Since we were city people, we approached this excursion with great enthusiasm and excitement—and our youngest son Thomas, at age three, was eager to catch his first fish. The five of us scrambled toward the small rowboat on serene and picturesque Dayton Lake in rural Michigan. Surprisingly, even with our five poles, tackle boxes and assorted fishing gear, we all somehow fit in the boat. Taking our positions, we now made ready to set off. As we began to use our none-too-familiar oars, we discovered, after about three minutes of strenuous rowing, that we weren't moving. Since the small lake was covered with water lilies, we as-

sumed we were just caught in their strong, thick leaves. But after rowing some more and seeing that there was still no movement, we all sat still to try to figure out the problem. One of us suddenly got it! We had forgotten to remove the rope that was holding us to the wooden dock. As soon as we lifted the rope off, we were free.

Is your teen free to sail? Why not release his boat from the home dock—or at least give the rope a little more slack? In a few short years, your teen will be out to sea by himself. Now is the time to ready his boat and show him how to maneuver in the adult world. You're going to need to help him out. You must be a teacher now. Just as we weren't really sure how to use our oars (as ridiculous as that sounds), it's best to assume he knows nothing about how simple household tasks should be done. Even though he has lived for thirteen years or more, don't assume he knows how to boil tea water, make a salad, hang a photo on his wall, change sheets, or fix a small car problem.

Teens can learn adult survival skills from the common, daily, mundane chores connected to their everyday lives—their personal, household, schoolwork, and social responsibilities. Be sure that all home chores transcend traditional gender boundaries. Young men need to cook, iron, and do laundry. Young women need to handle tools, change their car oil, and maintain yards. Let's look at some possible teen responsibilities. During the high school years, a teen can do the following: get up in the morning and be on time for school, part-time work, or personal engagements; juggle all outside commitments, including school, sports, and church and community activities; handle specific financial responsibilities, like managing savings and spending accounts; and do larger jobs on the home front, like shop for groceries and cook a meal, do the laundry, or take complete care of the car.

Younger teens of middle-school age (twelve to fourteen) can do the following: wash dishes and clean the kitchen after meals; hand wash the car; baby-sit siblings; keep their room clean; complete all homework; keep track of sports events, uniforms, and practice schedules; help with meal preparation; do outdoor yard work; and help wash the clothes. Of course, every family member is capable of performing basic personal responsibilities, which include making their bed, keeping their room relatively picked up, and all personal hygiene tasks (e.g., bathing, teeth brushing, etc.).

In keeping up with household chores, your teen will learn many valuable life lessons: Some tasks have to be completed right away. They can't wait. "We're all hungry, and it's your turn to fix the meal." Other tasks, if left undone, pile up. It's important to clean up after oneself, and it's necessary to do one's job so as to avoid inconveniencing others.

Teach teens that taking responsibility is the ultimate survival skill. Responsibility means living by one's word, and calling, if late, to say, "I'll be home soon." Responsibility means saying, "I made a mistake," even if one loses something because of it. It means earning privileges, not always demanding what one wants. It means paying if one breaks something.

It's best if you work together with your teen to transfer responsibility and know-how before he sets sail. Just as we became familiar with the how-tos of boating, teens need to learn the basics (heretofore performed by mom and dad) of keeping themselves afloat.

To teach adult survival skills, give your teens plenty of responsibilities around the house, and help them learn responsibility—the ultimate survival skill.

26

Maneuvering in the Adult World

Looking back on her own teen years, one mother recalled that she never felt she knew as much, at any other point in her life, as she did when she graduated from eighth grade (even though she had a masters degree from Stanford)! This explains why, as I mentioned earlier, teens hate advice: They think they know it all. But every once in a while, things line up and there will be a perfect opening for you to have a little input. Milk it! Look for opportunities (remember, timing is everything) to share a little knowledge, wisdom, or experience that will help your teen maneuver in the adult world. Let's take an example.

Both my teens wanted to learn how to get a salesperson to be

more flexible with "policy." Several times they felt their case or experience was unique, but couldn't find an understanding ear. In
one instance, my son ordered some computer equipment from a
PC warehouse to be used to connect two home computers together. When it arrived, he took out the cables and removed the
key part from its box. He installed it, but it didn't work correctly,
so he set it aside to try again later. After several more attempts, it
still didn't work. He called the warehouse to discuss the problem,
only to learn that they had sent the wrong part. They asked him to
mail it back. Ten days later, he received a letter saying that they
would not process the exchange because the packaging box had
not been returned with the part. If he did not reply, they would bill
him for the correct part. According to the letter, "no box" trans-
lated into his mistake, and he should pay again for the new part.

So I picked up the phone and asked to speak to the manager of the customer service department.

Anyone who works for the manager, I pointed out to my son, has no power to approach issues flexibly; they simply follow orders, policies, and rules. I explained to the manager what had occurred, using a very pleasant, honest, factual tone, blaming no one, especially her or her employees. I told her what had happened and asked if it would it be possible to accept the part without the box? I told her my son had mistakenly tossed the box out, as he assumed the correct part had been sent. Thankfully, she was understanding and responsive, agreeing to send out the appropriate part posthaste. This was an important lesson in navigating the mainstream of the adult world: Talk to the person who has the power to be flexible, and then be sure to treat them with kindness and respect.

Look for openings where you can teach your teen
how to maneuver in the adult world.

27

Behind the Wheel

How can you make the most out of teaching your teen to drive? First, if you currently do not hold any driving tickets, recognize that you are a good driver—and pat yourself on the back. You will need this self-acknowledgment as you begin the task ahead of teaching your teen to drive. In Illinois, in addition to the six hours of in-class instruction, new drivers must log twenty-five hours of behind-the-wheel, or in-car, practice with a person who is at least twenty-one years old. Most likely, this will be you.

One way to begin your teen's driving education is to try him out behind the wheel immediately. We think that since we drive every day, our teens are busily observing and absorbing our good driving habits. The extreme jerkiness of a teen's first attempts to steer—coupled with your growing panic as the car lurches and jerks along—should be enough to discourage you from embracing this experiential approach as the optimal teaching method. At the very least, you will note "considerable tension" between yourself and your teen. But more likely, you will fear for your life.

A better way to teach teens how to drive is to show them how to really see the road. Driving is a visual skill. Since we drive every day, we aren't aware of our own visual skills and discipline. For example, as I drive down the familiar residential street where we live, I constantly look ahead to check traffic, take note of any cars pulling away from their side parking spots, watch for any pedestrians who might cut across my path from both sidewalks, and then check for pedestrians who might be on the crosswalk at the approaching stop sign. I frequently check my rear view mirror for activity behind me. And I always look for fast-moving rollerbladers, bicyclists, and pets that might suddenly cross my path. In sharp contrast, a teenager drives down a street, focused on holding the steering wheel straight, accelerating and braking smoothly, and appearing cool. Compared to an experienced driver, their visual discipline and skill are extremely underdeveloped.

The task at hand then is to focus on the eyes in teaching your teen to drive. Say right out loud what you *see* as you drive and what you *do* to drive safely. At first, this narrative may feel strange, because you are talking about what you do automatically every time you sit behind the wheel. You may be surprised at how much seeing and doing actually occurs when you drive. For example, to turn left at a stop sign, say aloud: "Signal a left turn about one hundred feet before the intersection; start slowing down; stop completely in back of the limit line; look both directions for traffic; check for pedestrians who have the right of way; look ahead at the

vehicle travel path; and, before entering the intersection, look again in both directions for moving vehicles; now slowly enter and turn onto the street."

As you take time to describe each visual check, ask your teen to note the important role this plays in safe driving. The driver's eyes are active. This is a valuable lesson. Active eyes, coupled with lots of documenting and describing the driver's movements, lead to good teaching and good driving! Next, ask your teen to talk out loud as you drive, narrating what a good driver should be seeing and doing to drive safely. Listen as your teen describes your driving. Check for any omitted steps. Give feedback—especially positive, encouraging comments. When a teen can describe your good driving habits as you drive, you'll know that he is ready to get behind the wheel.

Now have him narrate as *he* drives. Again, listen and check to see if he has missed anything. Give feedback on both seeing and driving. If you approach it this way, he's going to know how to drive, all the way *through his body.* I mentioned this to my fifteen-year-old son James: "Driving has to be in your body." He looked at me with puzzlement and said, "I don't get it. What do you mean?" I replied, "It's sort of like your Swing dancing. You have to know the steps so well that when you hear the music, the steps are second nature, and you don't even have to think about them." Driving is the same way. The steps should become second nature so that you don't even have to think about them anymore.

As parents, our goal is to help young drivers achieve this body knowingness when it comes to driving—to help counterbalance the wild, impulsive style typical of most teens. When the body knows deeply how to drive, a teen can drive safely—and it can save lives.

Prepare your teen to drive so his "knowing"
behind the wheel is deep in his body.

28

Work Discoveries

During the summers when I was a teenager, I picked strawberries and beans at a nearby farm. Because my two older brothers had also picked berries and beans, I couldn't wait to begin. A bus gathered up the "pickers" every morning starting at 7:00 a.m. This was early, considering school was out and the summer was in full bloom. After stopping and picking up the entire crew, we arrived at the berry or bean patch about an hour later, each of us carrying a bag lunch to help us through the long day. We were paid five cents a box for strawberries, and two cents a pound for beans, and made about a hundred dollars from each over the summer. (By the way, these were 1961 labor wages.)

I recall many things—from a sore back, to the joy of stopping for lunch and eating outside, to the slope of the row in the berry patch as I worked my way down it. One of my most memorable experiences was the feeling of the wet vines early in the morning. The sun hadn't dried them off yet, and my hands felt cold and wet upon first touch of the lush vines. Like the lasting feelings of wet vines, these work experiences, when I was young, taught me a lot about the world of work.

When I was sixteen, I went to work in the local canning company, making a little over three dollars an hour. I worked this job for the next seven summers through college. One could pay for tuition through this factory work, by working three months in the summer. One bean season, I used a large pitch fork that had about forty separate prongs on it, to pick up empty cans and move them onto a conveyor belt. Another season, I inspected the local produce before it was put into the cans or cartons. As I got older and more experienced, I ran lab tests to inspect, grade, and record the quality of the fruit or vegetables, noting color, taste, and blemish specifications.

These jobs let me experience the world of work. The personal learning was rampant and formed much of my early thinking about work itself. It was hard work and boring at times, but it was work. This in itself was an important lesson: Work is work. If you stuck with it, the rewards were enough money to buy something you wanted. (My first summer picking berries I made sixty-six dollars. I wanted to buy a black-and-white TV, but only had half enough money.) Saving for college tuition became a priority. Probably the most difficult part of the canning factory work was missing the social or "play time" with other teens, when I worked the swing shift (3:00 p.m. to 11:00 p.m.) or the graveyard shift (11:00 p.m to 7:00 a.m.).

I think work is good for teens, especially summer work. Jobs during the school year should have reduced hours, no more than ten to fifteen hours weekly, so they don't interfere with school. It's important for the teen to find her own job. If a parent stays out of it, teens learn the difficulty of finding a job—an important discovery. Another is the experience of someone else serving as their boss, other than a familiar parent or teacher, to whom your teen must report and also be evaluated by at regular intervals.

Seeing how much money he or she can make, and what one can possibly do with this amount is critical to understanding value, expenses, savings, and profit. For example, if a teen works all day helping out in an office or serving as a summer camp counselor, then he can measure just how much work was required to earn that money. It gives him a feel for the hard work required, compared to the buying power of the money that was earned.

Other lessons are numerous: "I don't think I can do work that is boring day after day." Or, "I want work that brings me in contact with people, not machinery." Or, "I don't care what work I do as long as I don't bring it home. After-hours are for play, not thinking about work." Or, "I want professional work where I am treated with respect. This is very important to me." Or, "I want the freedom to decide just how I will spend the money that I have earned on my own." So, if your teen wants to try his hand at working, let him. Flipping hamburgers, baby-sitting, scooping ice cream, or helping out in the local toy store can lead to all sorts of unexpected discoveries. The memories, whether wet vines or sore backs, are deep and lasting.

Teens learn a great deal about the world of
work by experiencing it first hand.

29

The Spirit of Giving

There is an old Indian proverb that says: "Everything that is not given is forever lost." When we help teens find ways to be of service to their friends, family, school, and the larger community, we help them see the value of dedicating a portion of their lives to a larger purpose. Let's show them that they can make a significant difference—in themselves and in the world. Acts of kindness and service always bless the giver as well as the receiver. And they are never lost.

On the home front, show kindness to your spouse and each family member. Insist that siblings treat each other with kindness too. You may want to talk together—when the time is just right—

about the importance of kindness and what it looks like. It can be as simple as "Hi!," a smile, or "How are you feeling?" Discuss with your teen what it means to be kind. Look for ways to show kindness to another person who may be especially needy—a friend, a neighbor, or sick or elderly person—then take your teen along as you carry them out. Talk to your teens about their classmates. Is there anyone who needs a kind thought or act? How about the teen who is "different"? How about the classmate who is mean? Even if one doesn't feel like being kind, there is value in doing it anyway—because the kind act itself can change the feeling that follows. Help your teen see that kindness can make all the difference in someone's life, yet it's so easy to do.

A legacy of giving and service can begin now. A giving mindset says: Let me try to make the world more beautiful. It can be as simple as walking someone across a busy street or helping a friend study for an exam—or as difficult as speaking one's mind and conscience on a controversial topic or spearheading a campaign to offer a regular breakfast and shelter to the homeless in one's neighborhood.

Teens can give of their work, energy, time, and support. Many high schools require community service as part of their course requirements. These programs are important because they expose teens to the importance of giving to others within the community. Examples include: assisting in soup kitchens, reading to the blind, volunteering in hospitals, helping with physical rehabilitation needs, and tutoring younger kids with their homework. We can spread the spirit of giving through our own example. We can take teens out on community service field

trips, and encourage community service programs in schools that don't have them.

I know of one remarkable service effort that was identified and defined by the teens themselves. They called their group "Flowers on Friday." These fourteen-year-olds met frequently on Friday after school to bring flowers to people who were sick or needy. They purchased the flowers themselves at the local florist. One Friday, they visited the local hospital cancer wing and brought flowers to its patients. On another Friday, they gave their flowers to people on the street who looked as though they really needed something special in their lives right then. One woman they hand-picked for this reason said the last time she received a gift of flowers was over thirty years ago.

As parents, we can nurture an interest in giving and reaching out to others. Acts of service and kindness free us and our teens from self-imposed me-focused lives by widening our circles of compassion.

Encourage your teen to practice acts of kindness and to reach out to serve others. The spirit of giving transforms both the receiver and the giver.

30

✠

Relationships

When my husband and I were married, we wrote our own vows and selected readings from *Gift from the Sea*, my favorite book on relationships, to read during our wedding ceremony. The author, Anne Morrow Lindbergh, compares the stages of a relationship to various sea shells. Each shell offers guidance in relationship-making. Seeing each shell visually helps to understand the stage. (I keep a collection of these shells nearby.) I'd like to share what I think is an important message for parents to share with teens from a number of the shells.

The moon shell says solitude is good. Teens forget this need. Even though they may have serious relationships, finding time alone is helpful and healthy. The moon shell instructs teens to take time each day for contemplation, renewal, and quiet. Shaped like an island, the moon shell says to become islandlike—serene, self-contained, detached from the past and future, living in the present. Answers lie inside, and can only be discovered through centered, quiet living, especially when busy lives become fragmented. The moon shell whispers: "Find solitude, get away from your boyfriend or girlfriend, and become nourished and refreshed by distance—even if for a short while."

Most teen relationships are like the double sunrise shell. Couples are busy trying to make one world together. Each side of the shell, like the wings of a butterfly, is marked with the same pattern. A hinge binds the two together. They have perfect unity, with no responsibilities or burdens to worry about. There is a romantic bond between them. It is pure and unencumbered, magical and tranquil—no jobs, children, or worldly responsibilities. This romantic relationship is fleeting and fragile, as most teens will soon experience.

The oyster bed shell is irregular and uneven; it is not beautiful, but rather functional. This shell is easily found on the beach, but there are never two that are alike. Each shell is shaped and formed by an oyster struggling to survive. Its shell is untidy and spread out in all directions with encrusted materials attached to it to create a knobby look. The creature inside clings to a spot on a rock to make its home. Its essence is struggle. This requires finding a place to live physically, acquiring material things, and achieving a place in the world. There are many bonds, not just a romantic one, like in the double sunrise shell. An enduring, complex and intricate web is built between two people who are dependent on one another. There is the recognition that more is involved in loving someone than just gazing out at the sunrise together. Engaging in work, establishing roots, building a firm base, and becoming a part of the community all enter the realm of a loving relationship.

The last shell, the argonauta, is very rare. The moon shell, double-sunrise, and oyster bed are common beach finds, while the delicate argonauta can be found only in a store or a specialist's collection. Similarly, it is rarely found in the teen world, because relationships usually take a very long time to reach this stage. Still, its qualities are important to share with a teen, because it points to a future mark. The shell is white, transparent and feather-light to hold. The creature who used to live there didn't fasten itself to the shell at all, but rather used it to cradle its eggs until they hatched and swam away. Then the tiny creature sailed away, releasing its shell into the vast seas. Its essence is freedom.

Partners can hold on lightly, not tightly, and still create a pattern together that will nourish them both. This may be the most important lesson for teens to learn about relationships: There must be a pattern of freedom to find joy together. There should be no heavy hands, pressure, claims, or possessive touch. Holding on too heavily is caused by fear and self-doubt. Expose teens to the need for freedom within relationships, the value of relating to each other, whole and independent. For teens, and for all of us, this isn't easy. Teens see everywhere relationships where competition, domination, submission, and possession exist. The argonauta shell beckons to teens: look within to meet the deepest needs of your own nature. Through reflection, effort, and self-search, we discover our most profound inner resources.

Good relationships change and grow, with each phase
bringing new discoveries. Individuals need solitude,
quiet, and renewal (like the moon shell).
A good partnership is intimate and personal (like
the double-sunrise), functional (like the oyster
bed), and free and independent (like the argonauta).

31

※

Singing Heart—
First Love, Passion
and Sex

One of my favorite writers, Thich Nhat Nanh, says that the Vietnamese have two words that mean love, "tinh" (or passion) and "nghiā" (or faithfulness). When two people stay together for a very long time, they have "nghiā" It involves sacrifice and suffering, sharing joys, caring deeply, helping with difficulties, treating one another with respect, and looking after each other's well-being.

But your teen will most likely experience love in the form of "tinh"—and be blown over by its power. "I never realized how strong love is," said one teen. She continued, "It can't go away.

I've had it for eight months now, and I know I have to let go and move on. It's so hard. It's as strong as the love I have for my family." These are complex emotions for anyone, but a teen is experiencing them for the first time. While it sounds simple, as parents of teens, be guided by the knowledge that love is powerful. It can explain your teen's behavior when nothing else does. Romantic love is so all-consuming that your teen may think she has to set aside her love for family because she doesn't have enough love for both. Parents and siblings can feel this exclusion. She's sorting through her emotions now.

The topic of sex is very much on the mind of most teens. Don't think they aren't interested in talking about it. The most important thing you can do is talk. Start early. Get information in early. When they are eleven or twelve, begin talking. It's more important *that* you talk than what you talk about at this age, although topics should be simple and age appropriate. This establishes an openness between you and your child on sex-related issues. You want your teen to feel comfortable coming to you to talk later, and the best way to ensure this future dialogue is to initiate it early yourself. Let them know you welcome, are comfortable with, and like to talk about sex-related topics. Try to be nonjudgmental and open to their viewpoints, especially if they are trying out some new ideas or feelings on you. Honor their emotions and be willing to work through differences.

If you're not comfortable talking about sex—fake it. Comfort will grow with frequency. Ideally, if you started talking when they were younger, you'll be more comfortable talking as your child enters the teen years. If you didn't, there is no time like right now. So just start. Then, visit and revisit topics frequently. Your goal is to establish open dialogue on the subject along with regular check-ins: "What are you thinking these days about sex before marriage? Birth control? AIDS prevention?" These are good questions to ask your fifteen-year-old, if you've had conversations in the past.

Keep topics surfacing—frequently, lightly, and with openness. You'll find that your teen needs these conversations. They're on his or her mind now, and it's likely that not too many adults initiate discussion. Be sure to share your ideas and views on love, relationships, marriage—and even passion—with your teen.

Create an open dialogue between you and your teen to talk about love, passion, sex, and relationships.

32

Looking Ahead Together

Resolutions are simple statements of what we want to focus on during the year. They can serve as a beacon or road map to keep us on course in the time ahead. Of course, they can be done any time, but I think it is best to do them at the year's beginning. The start of the new year brings a freshness. If you encourage them within your family, especially early on, you may find that younger family members take the initiative to complete theirs, even before you do. (Our nine-year-old encouraged my husband and me do ours this year, and our two teens had already completed their lists of resolutions before our New Year's Eve celebration.)

We share them with one another at dinner on this night. Brevity is encouraged. Then it's easier to remember and focus on them throughout the year. We write them down individually and present them to each other. At nine, Thomas lists: read the *Hobbit* and the *Lord of the Rings;* remember to do my chores (sometimes I forget); try and do all of my homework at school, so evenings are freer; don't get head lice!; learn more magic tricks; and have *so much fun* in the summer. At fourteen, James lists: become an excellent Lindy Hop dancer; have a regular exercise program; read more during my free time; do some community service with some friends regularly, and have fun! At sixteen, John lists: live in the present; tell myself *everyday* what an awesome, great amazing person I am!; know that the impossible is always possible and set even greater goals for myself; know that it's okay to be silly or weird because there is no silly or weird thing—be free and unrestrained; trust my feelings, know they are always valid and that I am entitled to them; work out everyday; have fun; take swing; take kung-fu; become a Web master; read fun books; and improve my surfing. My husband lists: complete writing books; sell business; and enhance health. I list: promote my previous book; write my next book; rest; and have greater self-knowledge.

Resolutions give us permission to focus on what each of us thinks would be best for us during the coming year. Individually, we have greater say and involvement in the year's events. Sharing them with each other around the family table is an important annual ritual. It helps each of us have more personal interest, direction, and control over our own destiny.

Have your family write down their "resolutions" at the beginning of the year—and share them together!

PART 5

Connecting

33

Witches, Aunties, and Guides

I have a treasured friend who one of my teens refers to as "the witch." She has long, black hair and gives loving, perceptive guidance to young and old alike. We have a baby-sitter, Lisa, who is extraordinary when the going gets tough. Her perspective is invaluable because she has known our family for seventeen years. Our good friend Harriet has been helping us with household chores for seventeen years. We refer to her as "Yoda," and every family member seeks out her quiet, sage advice. She has taken a special interest in our teens, and they "listen up" when she has something to say. We also have several adopted aunties who play key roles in the lives of our teens—attending school, team, and ex-

tracurricular activities, and rarely missing a birthday party, holiday, or special event.

When these important individuals play a role in your teen's life, don't feel like you've lost your job. Rejoice! Welcome them into your family. Accept their support and the freedom and new perspectives they bring. Sometimes just the fact that it's not their kid allows outside adults to simply accept your teen the way he or she is, no changes necessary. These friends of the family, or "guides," can offer teens another shoulder to lean on. Someone else can help pick them up when you've lost your steam. Burdens can be shared—or even handed over to them for a period of time. And in times of dire need, they can just pray for you and your teen.

But beware. Know that "sharks" like to disguise themselves as friendly guides. Jump in like a flash when sharks enter the scene—people who want to harm or molest your teen, get him

hooked on drugs, or put him in real danger. Your role is clear: Guard your teen from harm, foul play, and injury. Go to bat for a teen to prevent abuse, maltreatment, and crippling damage, when your teen is in real danger.

But let teens go to bat for themselves when they are not in imminent danger. Play a more supportive advisory role when you ascertain that your teen has encountered a "jerk"—someone who, though hurtful and annoying, does not pose a serious bodily threat to your teen. A "jerk" can be anyone who exploits your teen's vulnerabilities, criticizes them too harshly, treats them unfairly, or acts in ways that are hurtful and annoying to your teen. It may be a psychologist who has a big degree to back up his recommendations; a seminar leader who sets a perfect trap to destroy your teen's self-confidence; a drama teacher who takes away your teen's role after she rehearsed, auditioned, and won the part; or a coach who humiliates your teen when he doesn't play well. Try to stay out of it. Stop practicing damage control. Yes, it's rough, but it's your teen's work. One of my sons discovered several "jerks" during a difficult period.

Let your teen know you are supportive of his decisions and moves. Offer suggestions if he asks for your thoughts or ideas on how to deal with the jerk. Listen to your intuition. If you feel strongly about something related to it (e.g., have an insight, a similar personal experience, or a hard lesson learned), share it with your teen. Never dominate or push. Know that your teen must figure out and initiate the steps to cope with the jerk. With jerks, your role is to be aware, watch, and, if possible, gently teach. Painful as it is to watch, your teen is learning about self-protection.

Nurture relationships with adults outside the family who take a supportive interest in your teen. Be vigilant for the harmful effects of "sharks", and gently support your teen's learning to cope with "jerks."

34

Play and Nourishment

I love music. I write with music blaring loudly, and I listen to tunes anywhere I can. This is especially true in my car, where I love to sing to a familiar song at the top of my voice—and even to those that aren't so familiar. I prefer a CD player while on the road, just because the sound quality is so good. In my opinion, sound technology is the most important feature of a car (after safety, of course). When my CD player broke down, I started listening to my oldest son's tape. This "mix," as he calls it, was carefully mastered by his own recording hand, as he transferred his favorite songs onto a blank audio tape. I can distinctly remember listening to his "mix" when he first completed it, and not liking it at all. But now, forced to make due until my CD player was fixed, I learned to like his music as much as my own. The lesson here is to be open to the things that bring nourishment to your teen. You might be surprised to discover that it does a lot for you too. And don't lose touch with what brings you renewal and joy. Parents need to be nourished too.

It's easy for adults to lose touch with the important role of play. I realized I had when I witnessed a group of six women, probably in their early forties, walking along the sidewalk very early one morning. With sleeping bags, pillows, and overnight bags in hand, they appeared to be returning from a "sleepover." Their tired eyes and unusually slow body movements confirmed this overnight get together. No one was talking. They all looked very content. This struck me as something that I hadn't seen, nor personally experienced, in a long time. While my own teens frequently have friends sleep over, in numbers, I can't remember when I last saw a group of women do this. I immediately thought of the book that I used to read to my children when they were little, called *When Grover Sleeps Over,* and I wondered if these women had eaten Monsterberry Crunch cereal in the morning or had packed up their pet goldfish to bring along to the sleepover. I imagined how fun it would be to get together with a group of my friends and talk into the night. What grand nourishment that would bring.

I think teenagers are better than adults at playing and seeking out what nourishes them. Ask them and discover what brings them enjoyment. My fifteen-year-old son has a simple formula for his play: get together with friends, hang out and talk, eat out, go to a friend's house, watch movies, listen to music. Every chance he

gets, he seeks out these activities. In fact, he pursues them with such vigor and focus that we know very little is more important to him right now than his group of friends. Let's take a cue from our teenagers and reconnect with our *own* sense of playfulness, and the things in life that bring us nourishment.

Remember to play, and make sure to connect with whatever it is that brings you nourishment.

35

Creating Families of Their Own

"They're only paying attention to their peers. That's their entire world—what their friends think about them. They don't want to be with their family anymore."

—one teen's mother

Teens are putting in lots of hours with their group of friends. As they become older, this time commitment gets even more demanding. Does this sound familiar? Do you remember wanting to be with your mother between the ages of fifteen and twenty-five? To receive my doctorate, I worked on a research project that let me see inside three groups of teens: a church group, a local YMCA group, and a drop-in hangout center. While I served as an adult advisor in each group, I also observed and interviewed nearly 150 teens and their advisors within the three groups. I felt as though I lived inside each teen group for one year. My research gave me a glimpse into the lives and interactions of teens that few parents are privileged to witness.

I did not find the alienated, dissatisfied, and unhappy teens that we so often read about in the press. Rather, in each of the three groups, the teens felt strong connections towards each other. In a sense, they created their own close "families." Teens learned how to be members of their groups, and to care for and maintain those groups. They learned how to interact with one another and take individual and collective responsibility for themselves, each other, and their activities—both planned and spontaneous. They learned to reach out and share their individual strengths and weaknesses with other members. Attached and involved, they created caring families through the daily drama of their interactions together.

Group members learned to mutually support and nurture one another too. I observed one teen who had gone through an awful experience. Although only one or two teens in the group knew what had happened, they all sensed that it had been something bad and offered their support when she returned to the group. Even though most of them did not know what the trouble was, they knew she needed help. As the adult staff member noted,

> "Incredible to watch, it was like some herd of animals, where one of them gets injured and the others crowd around and physically hold the one on its feet 'til it feels stable. You could just about see these kids crowding around her and

holding her up. The kids moved in on her faster than the staff did. In fact, I picked up from them the idea that something was wrong."

I witnessed this mutual supportiveness on another occasion, when another teen, Jimmy, had been kicked out of his parents' home. He lived in the streets for several weeks before the staff became aware of it. The teens had helped him with food, clothing, places to sleep, and moral support. At the point when he was really beginning to hurt, and they saw he was not going to be able to take it much longer, the teens informed staff. As soon as the teens were unable to help him further, they alerted staff, who then took over and began working with Jimmy's parents at home.

In both of these instances, and countless others, I observed teens taking responsibility for one another's welfare and offering tremendous support to one another. There was a very strong sense of looking out for each other in the group—just like in families.

Understand that your teen is not leaning on you, the parent, as much now. So when your teen gets involved in a group, don't worry that you're not important anymore. As your teen joins a small circle of friends, and spends large amounts of time with them, know that this focus is natural. Teens are learning how to care for each other in a group—a life lesson. Get out of the way.

Let teens shift to, connect with, and lean on their friends
now to create their own close "familes."

36

Becoming a
Group Member

I have been told that goats will give milk to people they like and withhold it from those they dislike. Teens are the same. Affection is carefully shared with a select few. Most teens are very particular about whom they admit to their inner circle of friends. For sure, teens value friends before anything else, including you. Peer relationships are everything. Friends are all-important. They replace the family, in some ways, as the place where daily relationships are played out, where meaningful interactions occur—the back-and-forth working through of ideas and events in the human drama.

Parents need to have greater sensitivity to how much work

it is for teens to join groups. Let's take a close-up look. As a new-comer, a teen must establish him- or herself to get accepted. This is not easy. Entrance can be negotiated through friends, relatives (e.g., brothers, sisters, and even cousins), and someone you are dating, if they are accepted. After the dating period is over, how-ever, the teen has to maintain the membership independently.

If teens don't know someone in the group, they can gain ac-ceptance by hanging around for a period of time, getting to know some of the members, and becoming involved with, and ac-cepted by, the other teens. Although accepted, this does not mean the other teens will quickly include them in what is hap-pening socially at all times. Most likely, the doors will remain closed for awhile, and they will have to find out about parties on their own. Regular members, however, are naturally "in on," or told about, parties.

I know of one group where the process of acceptance into the group involved some intricate bartering. To be accepted, there had to be a sense of give and take—the new person had to first do something for the regulars; then they would do something for him. At first, it was more important to be someone they could hit up for money, cigarettes, pop, or a favor. It was also important to be cooperative and get along and not judge the group. The new person had to accept the group before its members accepted him into it.

When a new teen comes into a teen group, there are certain things that other teens will communicate to him about the group. Older members or leaders will make very clear to the newcomer just what is and is not appropriate behavior. These leaders will even reprimand other kids when they do something unacceptable. The leaders help maintain the group in this way.

Don't make the mistake of trying to join these teen groups or trying to be a close friend to your teen. It just won't work. One parent had a strong point of view about whether to play the friend role:

> "I think parents should always remember they're parents and not friends. You are not a friend to your teen. I don't think you should be. I think too many parents strive to do that. And they can get into danger. I've fallen into that trap where I've just wanted to be friends with his friends. Because of course, I really don't feel 52, I really feel about 22 . . . because I'm just a young-at-heart chick. But I'm not. I'm a parent. You

know, and they don't want you to be friends with their friends. You're the parent. You're supposed to stay there and be the parent. And they'll do the friend thing."

Follow this parent's wise advice.

Know that becoming a member of a teen group is very difficult and time-consuming, and offer loving help and encouragement at every turn. But don't try to join your teen's group yourself!

37

Learning Leadership

"I've learned more here than anything at my high school. I'm responsible for everything (connected to our musical production). How well it goes depends on me. I have to make sure that everybody does what they're supposed to do. If they don't, then it will be bad, not only for this year's show, but the next one, too."

—a teen manager talking about his leadership role

Organizations are ideal places for teens to explore and practice what it means to be a group leader. I worked with fifteen teen leaders in a group called "the Board." They were responsible for putting on an entire music show. Each teen member had specific responsibilities to coordinate (e.g., tickets, lighting, publicity, etc.). There was also one teen manager in charge of the teen leaders, who described his own leadership role this way: "If the Board (of teens) doesn't do something, if one Board member doesn't do their job, then I'm responsible for that. It's really important to me that we make money on this show, that we have good publicity." He wanted to fire the teen Board member who was in charge of publicity because he felt this teen was not doing a good job. At one point, he also told the cast that they were not doing their job in helping to sell tickets for the play, defending his actions with: "I can't worry about what the teens (or the cast) think. My job is to tell them. I thought the peer pressure would get to me, but it didn't!"

Other Board leaders noted the difficulty they found with assuming an authoritative position among their peers, but they still carried out their leadership roles. They noted the importance of good communication among themselves (the Board) and the teens they managed, including leads, chorus, and crew, in the play. They all said that they had learned to talk with new self-confidence and to stick by their decisions. One Board leader described her newly acquired skills in the following way: "I've learned to take more control over a group of people that are working for me, and be more strict . . . plus, if I take on a lot, then I'll get other people to help me out."

Cast members also learned a great deal. One girl describes what she learned as follows:

> "You have to be less selfish and put others in front of you when you're working with other people. You really learn how to talk things out that go wrong because you can't work together if you don't. You also learn how to make sacrifices and

compromises. It helped me to be more aware of other people, how they feel and less how I feel."

Another member of the Board talks about the developing sense of community among the cast:

"They're getting more together, but it's still like 'I know my part and that's all that matters,' and you can't do that. You've got to be able to help people out and be able to say, 'Hey, you're singing the wrong note,' or, 'Hey, you've been late, why have you been late?' You've got to take the responsibility. The whole thing is taking everyone's responsibility and not just saying, 'Well, I'm here, I'm in costume, I don't care if she doesn't have a costume.' You've got to say, 'Hey, I've got a skirt or whatever.' I think that's coming more and more as the show goes on."

In group activities like planning this musical, teens learn how to be leaders, and take as well as teach responsibility. They need lots of opportunities to practice this role. Encourage your teen to join groups, clubs, organizations and activities to learn leadership. You will be amazed at their rapid rate of growth and maturation— and surprised at the talents that emerge.

Help your teen find groups where they can play positive leadership roles—and watch them flourish!

38

Beach Glass and Exploring

One of my favorite things to do is collect glass that has washed up on the beach. Low tide offers the best time for our leisurely search. We've learned too that there is more glass after a storm. Most all the glass has sides that have become smooth with time. We will occasionally find glass that is rough, but these pieces are rare. The movement of the ocean wears down the sharpness to create soft edges. Most pieces are brown, dark green, light green, or clear in color. Two years ago, I found one bright blue piece, and this year my son James discovered a small red one. We know these two colors are highly unusual, and we classify them in the difficult-to-find category, feeling highly honored to add them to our

collection. We keep all our glass in see-through jars, and look at them frequently inside our home. These containers, filled with our treasures, are prized by all. Not only do they remind us of our fun, but they take us back to the true pleasure and value of wandering and exploring, not really knowing what we will discover.

Teens love to explore and wander too. Experimenting and exploring serve as fine teachers. Think about the role of experimentation along a teen's path to adulthood. Recall and reflect back on your own journey. When you were a teen, did you sail straight ahead? Or did you take detours and side trips as you uncovered and learned more about yourself and your friends? The real excitement is the adventure and the discovery process itself. "We have to try this out" fits right in an explorer's mindset and to a teen's. Just as a storm brings more glass for us to find, often, more "treasures" are uncovered if the teen experience is a stormy one too.

As parents, it is helpful to visualize their end-state. Just like the glass with smooth edges, know that an adult will soon emerge. Visualize your teen with adult qualities. Hold an image of him being responsible and dependable. Interact with him as if he had these strengths. Don't forget to enjoy the journey. Experimentation will lead to mistakes. Remember that just as the rough edges of the glass are sure to be smoothed by the sea, your teen will, in due time, develop into a reliable, mature adult.

Keeping the end in mind is helpful, because the journey is colorful. There will be times when your teen has selected a friend that you don't think is right for him. (One of our teens has entered this area.) Know that he is *in the process* of learning about other people. His selection is teaching him something critically important about friendship, even though it may require a slight detour. Or if your daughter's grades have plummeted, get over the shock. Focus on the knowledge that she is becoming a more capable adult, but is just taking a side trip. Exploration, at this stage, is more important. The glass can become smooth, but it takes a very long time, wave after wave, to soften its edges. Teens must experiment in order to uncover the colorful treasures along their own path. Walk quietly beside them when you can, and find joy in their discoveries.

Visualize your teen in his adult end-state, and
find comfort from this view, knowing that
smooth edges aren't far away.

39

Mental Shift

As your teen gets older, you must make a mental shift. This is necessary to prevent conflict. But it is also important for a teen to learn how to handle fewer limits and more freedom. Keep in mind that if your teen starts living on her own after high school or goes off to college, there will be virtually unlimited freedom. It may help to think back to that period in your life when you experienced, for the first time, this new freedom. Be sure to recall that for many years, you were told when to return home at all points in the day, especially at night. While you might have negotiated this arrival hour with increasing finesse, in the end, it was still your parents' final approval of an agreed-upon time that defined your evening. But now, away from these imposed controls, your teen calls the shots. By the time you see your teen, after only a few

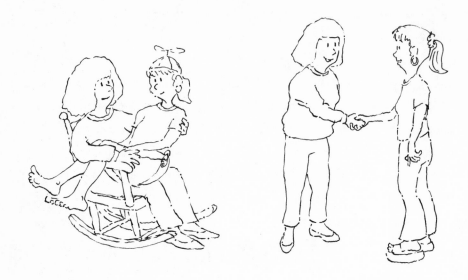

months living in an apartment or at college, she will have developed her own schedule and determined many of her own preferences. She will be, no doubt, proud of her abilities to handle these issues on her own.

Ease into these changes with greater amounts of freedom, slowly reducing the number and kind of limits you place on her while she is still with you. Three strategies are helpful. First, view and treat her as a young adult, not a child, and change your perspective to accommodate this new relationship. Second, *compromise* when there is a strong difference of opinion. Reach a decision that accommodates both sides. For example, if she insists on coming in very late, ask her to sleep downstairs so other family members won't be disturbed when she arrives home. And third, *encourage* your teen when signs of adult behavior emerge, and be enthusiastic about their newly acquired ways. These three strategies—viewing her as an adult, compromising in conflict, and encouraging mature behavior—can help you both make the mental shift, liberating teen and parent. Your teen needs to be freed from the demands of strict parental expectations. And you need to loosen up too. Then, you both can be free to create a new relationship between you. Do it. Consciously address making this change. You will experience stress and turmoil if you hold onto old ways. They can prevent you from experiencing a truly deep and special connection with the beautiful young adult who is emerging for you to get to know. Don't miss this opportunity. Swap the old "parent-to-child" for a new "person-to-person" relationship.

Make the mental shift. Enjoy the emerging adult,
compromise when conflict occurs, and watch
your relationship grow and change.

40

Self-Acceptance

Can your teen say aloud "I accept myself" or "I love myself"? When a teen has self-acceptance, she can yell out "I like myself just the way I am." Too many teens are brought up never to accept or like themselves. Self-acceptance—embracing, getting in touch with, and liking oneself—is vital to a teen. It says to take a gentle look at yourself and honestly enjoy and appreciate who you are. Rather than be tough and critical, it says to be easy, kind, and gentle with yourself. Uniqueness gives value. Differences are awesome. Help your teen to think this way and to be herself—without changing anything. She doesn't need to be thinner, smarter, faster, older, or more attractive. These "improvements" can be tossed out with the moldy bread. There isn't a perfect way to live a life. It's only perfect if it's right for your teen.

Each teen has certain qualities—voice, personality, looks, interests—and these give distinction. Teens can learn to love who they are, just as they are, inadequacies and all. This means they must take a close look at their essential "self," like what they see inside and outside, nurture a great love for their individual qualities, and learn to protect them. Parents can help teens discover this powerful life lesson: Other people can't make you feel inferior, unless you give them your consent. These are essential strategies for anyone. But accepting the self unconditionally is especially important for teens, when directions, feelings, or values are undergoing major shifts.

Fighting against self-criticism is a solitary pursuit. For a teen to discover that she is joyously wonderful is an internal journey. Each life has a drum beat all to its own. The bumps in the road, rather than the smooth stretches, are what make the trip dynamic and colorful. So, don't try to change your teen. Encourage her to become that unique individual within. Love her, just as she is, with all your heart. Acceptance is what she needs now.

As a new voice emerges from your teen, learn to appreciate its quality, whether playful or grave, forceful or hesitant, monotone or melodious, nasal or nervous, resonant or shrill. Its uniqueness gives it force and power. Your teen is becoming a star and learning how to sparkle. Let her know that you love how she expresses herself. With its inflections and interruptions, her voice is emerging—glorious, spectacular, unique. Encourage her full self-expression. Help her see her power, if you can. And finally, believe in her as she endures difficulties, and travels courageously along to reach her final destination—truly awakened with total self-acceptance and a deep sense of her own dignity and self-worth.

Accept and celebrate
your teen's emerging individuality.

Putting the Puzzle Together

For your convenience, the forty chapter summaries are collected below, spead out on the table again as a series of puzzle pieces from my heart to yours.

"LETTING GO" (Section 1) covers detachment. Pieces of this jigsaw picture include:

1. Because a new adult life forms, the family is sacred. But sacredness coexists with pain while your teen is detaching. Parents must love and let go simultaneously.

2. The pain of separation can be intense as teens grow into their individual destinies.

3. An argumentative teen is struggling to learn abstract thought and logic. Try to nurture, support, and even enjoy this development, rather than feel annoyed or threatened by it.

4. Parents can use the lessons of Taoism and tai chi to inform their parenting: Lead by letting teens follow their own nature and be their own guides; step back and allow negative force to pass by you, then return love; and conserve your energy for when you really need it.

5. Jump in fast when your teen is in big trouble, and practice lightheartedness and use humor for the smaller stuff.

6. A good sense of humor is an essential tool for surviving the teenage years.

7. As superteen takes flight, offer accurate information, hold out a safety net—and pray.

8. Like the turtle, with its four feet on the earth, remain sturdy and centered; be patient; learn to withdraw when necessary; and be sure to get adequate rest.

"KEEPING IN TOUCH" (Section 2) focuses on reaching in and discovering how to connect with your teen. Bits of insight I gleaned are:

9. A little attention to a teen's values early on can save a lot of head-butting down the road.

10. Parents can encourage teens to identify and prioritize their values—and share them as a family.

11. Teen's values are changing rapidly.

12. If you want to discover who your teen really is, observe, listen, and don't ask questions.

13. In talking with your teen, try these tips: Be available, tackle issues quickly, be open and honest, go easy on the unsolicited advice, and look for the good and acknowledge what you see.

14. Encourage teens to share their feelings with you—then validate them. Through your own example, demonstrate how to express emotions safely and effectively.

15. When it comes to the "Judge," a little work with the "Detective" can restore a teen's perspective.

16. Know that a self-reliant teen is able to identify strengths and list resources. This is a teen's buried treasure.

"EXPLORING" (Section 3) deals with teens' efforts to reach out, take risks, and test their (and your!) limits. Pieces of this picture include:

17. Things don't always go as expected, or as we would like them to ideally, but we can make the best of whatever we find and make the most of our time together.

18. Know that you aren't alone in trying to cope with a rude, cantankerous teen. Try to meet with other parents for support and an exchange of ideas.

19. Teens want to do it all themselves. Let them!

20. Help teens learn the tools to chart their own life course, so they can begin to find their way—if they should ever find themselves "lost in the dark."

21. Give your teen the freedom to choose and the power to act, and be sure to support his decisions, even when they are life-altering.

22. When parents let their teens experience mistakes, they discover, learn, and are nourished through hard-won lessons.

23. Become aware of what popular drugs are available in your area, share precautions with your teen, and encourage recreational activities that are fun, people-oriented, and positive.

24. Be sure to set reasonable boundaries to protect your family culture. Give your teen a key role in setting the boundaries; communicate clearly what the boundaries

are, through written and verbal reinforcements; execute the consequences of broken rules; and up the ante when necessary.

"ACQUIRING SKILLS" (Section 4) deals with learning essential adult survival skills. Pieces of this jigsaw picture include:

25. Give your teen plenty of responsibilities around the house.

26. Look for openings where you can teach your teen how to maneuver in the adult world.

27. Prepare your teen to drive, so his "knowing" behind the wheel is deep in his body.

28. Help teens learn about the world of work by experiencing it first hand.

29. Encourage your teen to practice acts of kindness and to reach out to serve others; the spirit of giving transforms both the receiver and the giver.

30. Good relationships change and grow with each phase, bringing new discoveries. Individuals need solitude, quiet, and renewal. A good partnership is intimate, personal, functional, free, and independent.

31. Create an open dialogue between you and your teen to talk about love, passion, sex, and relationships.

32. Have your family write down their "resolutions" at the beginning of the year—and share them together.

"CONNECTING" (Section 5) is about getting closer and relating to others and oneself. Bits of insight I gleaned were:

33. Nurture relationships with adults outside the family who

take a supportive interest in your teen. Be vigilant for the harmful effects of "sharks" and gently support your teen's learning to cope with "jerks."

34. Remember to play, and be sure to connect with whatever it is that brings you nourishment.

35. Let teens shift to, bond with, and lean on their friends, creating their own close "families."

36. Know that becoming a member of a teen group is very difficult and time consuming. Offer help and loving encouragement at every turn. But don't try to join your teen's group *yourself!*

37. Help your teen find groups where they can play positive leadership roles—and watch them flourish.

38. Visualize your teen in his adult end-state, and find comfort from this view, knowing that smooth edges aren't far away.

39. Make the mental shift: Enjoy the emerging adult, compromise when conflict occurs, and watch your relationship grow and change.

40. Accept and celebrate your teen's emerging individuality.

ABOUT THE AUTHOR

Susan Smith Kuczmarski, Ed.D., is an educator, lecturer, and sociological authority on families and culture. She is the author of two previous books, *The Family Bond: Inspiring Tips for Creating a Closer Family,* published by Contemporary Books in 2000, and *Values-Based Leadership,* published by Prentice Hall in 1995. Trained as a social scientist, Dr. Kuczmarski has done extensive research on how children learn social skills and how adolescents become leaders. Over the last twenty-five professional years, she has taken high school teens on leadership-building retreats, taught younger teens in inter-school workshops, and instructed college teens to help sort through their values and future directions. She holds a Doctorate in Education from Columbia University in New York City, where she was named an International Fellow. She conducts frequent workshops and seminars for parents and educators, and has been interviewed about familymaking on radio and television.

Dr. Kuczmarski has taught at seven universities, worked in three nonprofit educational organizations, including the United Nations, and co-founded an innovation consulting firm, Kuczmarski & Associates, in Chicago. She holds two additional master's degrees in sociology and education from Columbia University, has been listed in *Who's Who in the World* for the past twelve years, and was recently selected for inclusion in *Outstanding People of the 21st Century* and *500 Leaders of World Influence.* She lives in Chicago with her husband and three sons, ages 12 to 18. To obtain information about workshops and speeches contact the author at: www.sacredflight.com.

INDEX